While The Candle Burns

While The Candle Burns

Poetry and Prose

By

Judy Barrat

ISBN # 1-890799-45-9
In association with The Writer's Corner

DEDICATION

This book is dedicated to
Randi Barrat and Y.B. Barrat,
my most inspiring creations

and

to my many friends and family
who have consistently encouraged
and supported me.

ACKNOWLEDGMENT

Grateful acknowledgment
goes out to my very patient editor/organizer,
Carole Boyce who has so much more
than patiently and diligently worked
with me on this book.

FOREWORD

*Will my words, my pictures resonate with
anyone or will yesterday's childish rhyme
prove to be today's metaphor for madness?*

Judy Barrat's work speaks to the frailty of human
nature. Her poems illuminate how laughably vulnerable
the human race can be. The quote above comes from
her poem, "What's To Be Done With The Words," which
is truly about more than words. This poem, like many of
Judy's poems, is about being a mother, a woman, a
human.

I met Judy when I started the Canyon Poets poetry
reading a few years ago. Since then, I have spoken to her
close to every week. She has shared a tremendous part
of her life and her poetry with me, and for that, I will be
eternally grateful. Judy is a quiet force. She will come to
a reading and sit quietly, and then when it is time to
share a poem, she will share something so true to life, it
makes anyone who is listening forget about the petty
trivialities of their own life. Her work taps into what is
truly important with a sense of style and lyricism that I
rarely see in any other poet.

*And the music continued to play in my head;
it played while the room emptied, as I got
into my car and drove away*

The first thing I noticed about Judy's work was its
narrative nature. She tells a story and paints a picture in
the most unique ways. There have been multiple times
when listening to her read her work that I got lost in her
words, and she takes me to a different place. A lot of her

work has a brightness to it, even her darkest works carry a sense of hope.

> *Now in your eyes*
> *I see that question reflected*
> *and know it was real, if only for a moment.*
>
> *Oh yes, I remember,*
> *and I search*
> *for nothing less will suffice.*

There is no question that Judy Barrat's work will stay with you like a lost lover, her verse will tuck its way into the corner of your mind and take up residence in a comfy armchair. A lot of poets mirror their own lives in their works; Judy's work mirrors society. You can see it in her fantastical poem about Cupid to her natural poem "Kauai."

Judy's work blows me away. After a particularly inspired day, I heard one of Judy's poems, and I said to her, "Judy, you need a book. Make it happen!" I am glad she did.

Katerina Canyon
Author of Surviving Home

PRIOR PUBLICATION CREDITS

Quill & Parchment:
The Beach
Vigilante

Alta Dena Literary Review:
The Cloud Rider

World Enough Writers-Beer, Wine & Spirits Anthology:
Coffee For Wine

San Gabriel Valley Poetry Quarterly:
I Am
To Grandma's House

Village Poets Anthology:
Remembering the Daisy Days

Sadie Girl Press--Then & Now Anthology:
The Road

LAPWC Anthology:
Ballet Naturale
There Is No Silence

Overseas Adventure Travel Newsletter:
Chefchaouen

Scenes of SoCal, Directory of So Cal Poets –
Finding Light

Spectrum Magazine *(multiple issues)*
Where Do They Come From
Then and Now
Norma
Suspended
One For The Road
Holiday Visit
After
Noir Night
You And Me
The Pain Of Success
Walls And Doors

Spectrum Blogspot *(online)*
Click
Precious Things
Summer
The Arrival

California Quarterly:
I'm Sorry Mr. Webster

California State Poetry Society:
I'm Sorry Mr. Webster
The Road
The Beach
I Am

Quantum Entanglement:
I Feel You

Sensual Southern California Erotic Poetry:
What Was That?
Like David

Rhythms of Southern California:
Insomnia
Imagine A Land

Blue & The Blues Anthology:
Chefchaouen
I Can't Sing The Blues

Once Upon A Poem Anthology:
A Blank Page
Sometimes
Writing
Where Do They Come From?
There Is No Crime In Rhyme
Blocked

TABLE OF CONTENTS

While The Candle Burns

WHILE THE CANDLE BURNS

In the dark
the light of a single candle
no matter how small
can be precious and magical

When flame is put to wick
on a simple stick of wax
the shadows cast
as it dances in the stillness
are a reminder
of the elusive ephemeral
nature of all existence

While the candle burns
we dream our lives
and hopefully live our dreams
as it casts its shadow
on whatever walls surround

And we dance like the flame
as the winds of time direct
in the dark but also in the light
And we write our own stories
the happy the sad the good the bad
the magical the fantastical
and we fill them with words
and colors directly from our hearts

All this we do—
while the candle burns

****

WORDS

SOMETIMES

Sometimes they flow free
as a cool mountain stream
that refreshes tired feet
after a long day's trek

Sometimes they enfold
gentle and nurturing
like a hug one desperately needs
when sadness overwhelms

Sometimes they entrance
and seduce with a touch
tender as a lover's caress
until nothing exists but desire

Sometimes they bring tears
when least expected
by evocation of a joy or sorrow
long forgotten or merely anticipated

Sometimes they spew forth
like lava from a volcanic eruption
and decimate everything in their path
in an irretrievable instant

Sometimes they pierce so deeply
a heart is driven to such despair
it clings to life from a distance
too difficult to traverse

Sometimes they breed hate
Sometimes they inspire peace

And sometimes they fill life
with beauty and color
more vivid than ever imagined
Sometimes—if we let them . . . words
******

WHAT'S TO BE DONE WITH THE WORDS

I've often been distracted by words
unconnected unrelated words
rattling around in my brain
and random pictures flashing
floating through my mind.

So absorbed in the attempt
to make sense or sentence
of this muddled mélange
of mental mayhem I barely
noticed the world around me:
the tree on my neighbor's lawn
yesterday a scraggly sapling
today a majestic maple
or the yard down the street
once all dirt and weeds
now a tropical paradise.

As winter slithered into spring
and I wrestled with the words
coming fast and furious but formless
I watched my toddlers take giant steps
to university, master's degrees,
marriage, and more.

And I wondered:
What's to be done with the words?

Will they halt the havoc in the world?
Can I splash them on a canvas
like a Pollock painting
and swish them around
into something someone
might perceive as profound?

Might they explain why when we hear
of a crime, a death, an accident or illness,
we simply shrug our shoulders,
cluck our tongues or shake our heads
but a frisky puppy, a laughing infant,
or a simple show of kindness,
brings tears to our eyes.

Will my words, my pictures
resonate with anyone
or will yesterday's childish rhyme
prove to be today's metaphor for madness?
Perhaps it already has.

Or, maybe as the song says,
"Love is the answer,"
and maybe it doesn't even matter
what the question is because
everything is better with love—
everything—even—no especially . . . words.

****

I'M SORRY MR. WEBSTER . . .

but I must take issue with your
authority as to two words you deem
synonymous which in my view
are not as interchangeable
as your famous book professes:

The words I refer to if you please
are "naked" and "nude." At the risk
of appearing argumentative sir,
no one visits art houses to view
famous "nakeds."

It is the "nudes" those entrancing
figures of women and men unclothed,
baring their bodies that we seek.

So, you see "nude" is art—in the proper
setting; and, in an improper setting
which I will leave to your imagination,
"nude" may still be art though it may
simply be embarrassing or even criminal.

"Naked" on the other hand I believe
is more synonymous with "exposed"
for "naked" is so much more than
baring the body. Naked is devoid
of the mythic mask one might wear
to hide the truth of oneself from
the world—the pain, fear, shame
or insecurity.

Oh, Mr. Webster, I have never seen
some of my friends unclothed
and may never, but I have seen them
naked, stripped of armor and shield

which enable them through each day.
I have seen in their eyes unshed tears
which bespeak hearts that ache with
the pain of caring too much or perhaps,
not enough.

However, sir, I concede that
in personal relationships,
nude is so much more delightful
when both parties are naked.

****

WRITING

It may be meant to entertain
or be exquisitely profound
It may reveal a hidden soul
or totally confound

It may induce intense emotion
or help one to unwind
It may be set to music
or paint pictures in the mind

It may be boring to a fault
or inspired and erotic
It may lack color and imagery
or be completely cinematic

It may be candid and sincere
or fallacious and deluded
It may shock someone conceived it
or make you wish that you did

******

IN DEFENSE OF RHYME

These days it's unacceptable
in circles literary, and in fact
the literati find it quite incendiary
to hear a poem with rhythm
though its words be so sublime
as to make a strong man quiver
and even worse, with rhyme

For lovers of more fire and flare
amorphous prose is not enough
so, they blithely write their rhythmic
verse and ignore such harsh rebuff

Bathe gently in the flow of words
Let your heart and mind engage
Hear the rhythm of the poet's heart
that beats upon the page

****

A BLANK PAGE

There it is before me
stark and white
as new-fallen snow
like an empty face
devoid of expression.

It waits for me to make
the first mark of life
to graze its surface
give it expression
make it reflect joy or love,
sadness, fear or anger.

This inanimate spiritless
blank sheet of paper
like an unborn child, waits
to be brought into the world
kicking and screaming
or cooing and gurgling.

And I . . . am I to be a midwife
who cares only that this child
be delivered with as little pain
and drama as possible?
Or am I to be a mother who
will nurture and groom it
in the hope it will be beautiful
and smart, insightful and artistic
and funny at times—humor is important.

I feel something stir in my mind
and a gentle twitch in my hand
which grows more persistent.
I think it is coming, emerging—
a first tiny utterance then another

one by one they come in spurts
and stop, then more and more.

I'm overwhelmed with feelings.
Is this love so instantaneous
before it has arrived complete?
And now it's here—not as big
and strong as I had hoped
but delicate and sweet
and full of life and potential.

I must give it a name.

I shall call it . . . Poetry.
And when it is stronger
I will send it out into the world
to touch minds and hearts
as it is meant to do.

******

BLOCKED

I'd been sitting in my chair so long
    my bottom was getting numb
I'd thought myself a writer
    but the words just wouldn't come

I conjured up scenarios
    both fantastic and absurd
that played so clearly in my head
    but I couldn't write a word

Scenes from early childhood
    ran rampant in my brain
Surely a curly-haired dimpled kid
    would spark a sweet refrain

Memories of great romance
    both fantasized and had
still left me with my pages blank
    frustrated and sad

I flirted with the Zen of dance
    thought erotica divine
My parts began to vibrate
    but I never wrote a line

I contemplated vast blue seas
    green hills in all their glory
but even nature's majesty
    did not inspire a story

My thoughts moved to clandestine plots
        in locales far from home
and fascinating though they were
        I wrote no thrilling tome

I've survived countless sleepless nights
        over all this wasted time
with naught to show for my effort
        but this silly little rhyme

****

FINDING LIGHT

Some dreams are best had
in the darkest of days
Waking dreams of brighter times
that fill me with hope
for fulfillment of longings

All I want to do is write a poem
and I kick myself for my
current lack of inspiration

I walk for hours in the woods
feel the earth soft beneath my feet
listen to birds sing and wish
such beauty came so naturally to me

A squirrel runs up a tree
The leaves rustle and dance
My mood begins to lift as I watch
shadows shimmy as shards of sunlight
beam between branches

I become acutely aware that
I will never write a poem to match
the beauty of Mother Nature

But I sure as hell can try

****

WHERE DO THEY COME FROM?

They come from nowhere it seems
but also, from anywhere, everywhere:
a thought, a picture, a word, then another.

They conjoin like sperm and egg
to grow and expand within us,
come to life and in time emerge
as something beautiful or interesting
or hopefully . . . both.

We nurture, feed, mold, play
and work with them until
one day we proudly claim them
as our own; then send them,
our children, into the world
to inspire and arouse,
bring laughter or tears.

From a thought, a picture,
a word, then another,
from nowhere, anywhere,
everywhere, they become

our poems,
our stories,
our children,
our hearts.

****

THERE IS NO CRIME IN RHYME

No one flinched when the masters did it
with tales of love, art, or history
Not a soul in those days forbid it
Why folks do now is a mystery

The Roberts did it eloquently—
Mr. Service and Mr. Frost
in stories they told so reverently
with no detail or emotion lost

Lord Byron, Shakespeare, Keats and Poe
told tales in rhyming verse
Yet poets today eschew their flow
and think nothing could be worse

Coleridge's Ancient Mariner Rime
Longfellow's Hiawatha
are epic masterpieces so sublime
Who dares to fault these authors

Dickinson, Whitman, Shelley, Millay
delivered perfection every time
And no substance did they allay
by their brilliant use of rhyme

Some poems may indeed be trite
Eloquence takes thought and time
But it's proven though protest you might
there is no crime in rhyme.

****

MUSIC
&
DANCE

THE SONGS I'D LIKE TO SING

Oh, the songs I'd like to sing
if only sounding good were a thing
I could at least be mildly sure of
in which case folks would hear
much more of all the things I have to say
in poetry, stories, and songs—
         OY VEY!!

But sadly that is not the case.
Though I might sing a line or two with grace,
what I hear in my head is not quite the same
as what springs from my mouth—
         it's really a shame.

Folks tell me:
         "Patience, practice . . . give it some time.
         Don't sit around writing frivolous rhyme."

I have nightmares about how I'd find the right key
and that Florence Foster Jenkins
         would have nothing on me!

If I could, I'd sing the song Joe Raposo wrote
(which by law, I cannot quote)
It implies, though some don't think I should,
         sing anyway if it makes me feel good!

****

FLAMENCO

Down the narrow aisle he walked, tall, slim, proud; a guitar slung over his shoulder, hung at his back. His long, dark hair rested on the shoulder of his troubadour coat, its nubby fabric in contrast to a face smooth and delicate of feature, which bespoke an artist's grace.

He reached the small stage, removed his coat, revealing a brocaded vest, a loose white shirt with full sleeves fitted at the wrist, an open collar with a white ascot fastened with a black pearl stickpin. His trousers, of the same nubby fabric as the coat, hung over worn brown leather boots. He lifted his guitar.

Sitting cross-legged on a tall wooden stool, left ankle resting on right knee, guitar balanced on top, he spoke in a gentle voice of how his flamenco guitar differed from a classical: how the woods of which it was crafted were fit together to create a sound or timbre different from other guitars and of these things he spoke as though we had asked—and with the certainty that we wanted to know.

He began to play. His fingers danced up and down the full length of his guitar so fast they appeared not even to touch the strings. He slapped the wood and played the chords as with closed eyes he threw his head back in rapture.

I closed my own eyes and saw him even more clearly and heard the music as though I had never heard music before, and when I looked up his eyes met mine with an unwavering gaze, and in that moment, I knew that he knew I felt his passion too.

With lightning speed, he strummed the last chords, jumped off the stool, and with boot heels hitting the floor he arched his back, raised his guitar in the air, and shouted "OLE!" as the crowd rose to its feet clapping and stomping and screaming for more while I—I stood in the aisle, immobilized by the magnetic heat of his gaze as he stepped off the stage and slowly made his way toward me . . . .

I held my breath. I could still hear his music in my head, slower now, one note at a time, the strum of each string resonating in my body, setting me on fire. I was aware of his every movement as he walked up the aisle—the slight lift of his shoulder to shift the guitar to a more comfortable spot, the hint of a smile as he acknowledged the applause and obvious appreciation of the crowd as he passed, the splay of the fingers of his left hand as it moved up to brush a hair from his face . . . the glint of a gold ring on his third finger . . . perhaps I was mistaken.

I looked again at those piercing eyes, still focused like laser beams but not at me—just beyond; and as he passed, completely unaware, his shoulder brushed mine and I turned to see a young woman just behind me, tall and slim with dark curly hair and porcelain skin, her clear blue eyes beaming with pride. She smiled, then laughed out loud with unbridled delight, her arms spread wide, waiting for him to enter the circle of her love. It was beautiful . . . perfect.

And the music continued to play in my head; it played while the room emptied, as I got into my car and drove away.

Flamenco, full of excitement and passion!

****

BARON OF THE BASS
 (For Michael Saucier)

Those of you who know him
will recognize his face
His talent speaks quite clearly
as he strums and bows his bass

That big bass fiddle by his side
might look like an antique
But when he starts to work it
Man! He makes that fiddle speak

He gets completely swept away
yet never breaks a sweat
When he vocalizes while he strums
It's a stunning bass duet

He's tall and slim, a friendly guy
He doesn't drink or smoke
but might easily have started
on that night his G-string broke

An intense expression filled his eyes
but he compensated well
and if any notes were missing
not a soul could tell

He strummed the three strings he had left
no angst showed on his face
He sang and played as always
because he's the Baron of the Bass.

****

JAZZ – IT'S PERSONAL

Jazz . . . it's personal.
It's all about how YOU hear it
Maybe it starts with the bass
Its heartbeat pulses through your veins
along with your blood
and you feel a unique aliveness

Soon the piano comes in
first smooth and melodious
then builds in passion
and takes off with wanton abandon

as the drums set a velocity
that makes you move and vibrate
Before you realize your head starts to bob,
and your fingers tap on the table

Then from some ethereal place
comes the waah-waah of a trumpet
which tears at your heartstrings
with its mournful cry

The strum of a guitar eases in
each note so distinct it feels
like the sweet tingle of a raindrop
and sends shivers up and down your arms

just as a trombone starts to speak
in a voice so smooth and soothing
it's almost hypnotic

You close your eyes, sway like
a reed in the wind

when a sudden low sensuous
almost predatory growl
is emitted from a tenor saxophone

Unconsciously you tug at your collar
start to unbutton your shirt
The notes flutter and tease
and ascend into a long high feverish wail
until you simply want to rip your shirt off altogether

But that's just me—
What's it like for you?

******

I CAN'T SING THE BLUES

When some folks are sad
        they sing about it
I would do that
        but I doubt it
would have the same
        effect as those
who have melodious voices
        to describe their woes
in words and stories
        that are so direct
and honest
        they demand respect
Their tales of hurt
        their plaintive tone
the heartbreak of
        being left alone

For instance:
Jane is as blue as she can be
Her man has gone away
He's left her for someone new
She can't face another day

So, she sings about her heartache
Wonders what she's going to do
The music comes from deep inside
and helps her to get through

Or perhaps:
John's blue because he lost his job
Can't survive without his pay
He never saved to make the rent
Just lived from day to day

So, he sings about his troubles
and decries his injured pride
And the woman he loves just told him
she will never be his bride

Oh, it fills my heart to hear the words
those blues singers define
Hell, it almost makes me wish
the pain they feel is mine

Now I'm not broke
        or brokenhearted
I've got a job
        No one's departed

My kids are grown
        and doing great
I've got my health
        and a decent mate

My rent is paid
        My car runs well
I'm not in debt
        My life is swell

But I've still got the blues.
I'll tell you why

If I could have just one more thing
to sing is what I'd choose
You see, I can't sing to save my soul
I've got the I can't sing the blues blues.

****

CARLOS NAKAI'S MAGIC FLUTE

I fell asleep to the enchanting fluidity
of Carlos Nakai's flute and dreamed
of a deep, thick forest.

In a clearing where beautiful dark-skinned
people were gathered around a fire,
a young man played a flute. The haunting
tone spoke of an anguish that saturated
his soul; its staccato gasps and subsequent
wails expressed more than words ever could.

The people around the fire joined hands
and swayed slowly to his music, first
to the left then to the right, like the ebb
and flow of a tide, their movement absorbing
the searing sorrow of the young man's soul.

He played as if in trance; tears flowed freely
from the unfathomable depths of his dark eyes
which stared, unseeing, perhaps into his future.

A grey wolf appeared at the edge of the woods,
stood still by a tree, ears rigid as if listening
to the mourn of the flute. The wolf cocked its head
to one side for a moment, then slowly passed
through the circle to sit beside the young man.

Subtly, the music changed, became lighter, smoother;
the notes fluttered like a breeze through the trees,
morphed into a sweet refrain then receded
into total silence . . .
        except for the whisper of leaves.

******

LILLIANNE

The first I heard of Lillianne
was as I walked along the Seine
when suddenly I heard music
from nowhere I could see.

I stopped a woman passing by
and inquired: "*D'où vient la musique*"?
The surprised lady laughed and in English said,
"Ahh, you hear it? This is Paris's great mystique.

"It is said the child Lillianne,
a flower vendor's daughter,
as a teenager, sang and played accordion
as she walked here along the water.

"She strolled the streets of gay Paris
from the gardens to the Eiffel Tower
and to the Louvre and Notre Dame bridge
where she sat and played for hours.

"Many people think they've seen her,
though none can say for sure
Some claim a ghostly image of her
hangs just inside the Louvre's front door.

"But when Notre Dame Cathedral burned
and flames tore through its core,
there was no further sound from Lillianne;
her music came no more.

"It is said Notre Dame will be renewed;
all its beauty will survive.
And if today you heard the music,
Lillianne's spirit is still alive."

****

THAT NIGHT

It was out there on the highway, Lincoln, I think, not far from the beach; a medium-sized bistro—nondescript exterior and inside, a Greenwich Village coffee house vibe. Decent food, burgers and such; wine and beer too.

Colored lights hung from driftwood beams on the ceiling and walls—kitschy—gone now, all of it, like it never existed, or maybe in a dream. It sure seems like a dream.

But that night about seven years ago, it was alive! Those colored lights turned to the center of the stage to spotlight a bulky Bohemian-looking woman with dark straggly braided hair, a big round face, ruddy complexion and more than a hint of mustache. Long strands of marble-sized multicolored beads dangled from her neck over the front of a purple tent-like dress, its deep V-neckline threatening to expel at least one pendulous breast every time she moved even just a little.

But no one cared, because when she began to sing, the sound that emanated from her lips was so ethereal, all movement in the room ceased. Not a whisper nor clink of glass could be heard, so hypnotic and angelic was her voice.

A momentary, almost stunned, silence followed her final song and then a thunderous roar of appreciation so loud the building vibrated.

People kept talking while she introduced the next act; no one paid attention. But in a minute, the intentionally discordant sounds that came from the guitar of the guy at the microphone made them look up. He stood there watching them from beneath the slightly tilted black fedora on his head. Steel grey eyes, sharp and watchful, slightly amused but not unkind—sort of wolf-like, roamed over the crowd. He grinned, or maybe it was a scowl; it was hard to tell.

He had pale skin, an average build, perhaps five foot ten and was dressed in black jeans, and a black vest over a burgundy T-shirt. His face bore a stubbly growth of brownish beard.

Totally at ease standing on the stage, he strummed a few chords, adjusted the strings, strummed again and began to sing. His raspy, gravelly voice was almost mournful, the tune unfamiliar . . . poetry really, kind of bluesy, honest and deeply heartfelt about everyday life, how it flows . . . the beauty and wonder, pain and suffering. The chorus was so catchy and arresting, the crowd spontaneously began to sing along, the words unimportant, the melody so instantly ingrained in their consciousness they couldn't help themselves. One tune after another—originals, he said, pieces of his life—each one more memorable than the last.

And then it was done, time to go back to the real world, to home, wherever and whatever that was.

I never heard of either of them after that night; wonder what happened to them. The place disappeared—torn down; as I said, like it never existed. Maybe it WAS all a dream. Maybe.

But damn! I can still hear those voices.

****

THROUGH IT ALL

Perhaps it was too soon
to be out in a crowd
too soon after the end
of her "forever" love.

In the darkened theater
she waited to hear
the magic she was told
this young man created
when he sang.

 He began.

It was just another song
about the pain of lost love
sung by a man too young
to know of such things.

Still, as she listened, she was sure
he had lived another lifetime
to sing this song
with such intense emotion.

Her eyes devoured each nuance—
thrust of chin, blink of eye, toss of hair.
She learned him, absorbed him
deep in her soul as if from centuries past.

She heard each word
each inflection
as story unfolded, cinematic
and she listened:
through the words

through the tears
through the pain
through it all
back to love.

And in the dark
eyes now closed
she sensed his movement
across the stage
perceived each smile
arch of brow
and her heart received
the clear message
of his lovely words:

One thing ends
One thing begins
Night gently melts
into new dawn
Love will find you
even when you're lost.

Just stand still.

******

JAZZ + 2 GLASSES OF WINE

You have your radio tuned to a jazz station
and just catch the end of a Miles Davis solo
when a tune you've not heard before begins.
You're alone in your office, standing in front
of your computer. You have a gizmo
on your desk that raises the computer
to eye level so you can type standing up.

You steadily sip your second glass of grape
while you try to think of something to write
because you want to have something new,
something jazzy to present to your friends.
Stray thoughts slowly seep from your fingertips
to the keyboard and onto the screen.

Soft piano music, sort of tinkly and watery
but kind of jazzy, sneaks up on you from behind
and traces the entire perimeter of your body
up one side, over your head, and down the other
and you feel that outline like a wave of piano keys,
all tinkling somewhere up around the High C.

The big bass fiddle starts to speak in a low,
throaty pulse tone that your brain doesn't
quite translate but your body does, and it begins
to move; your weight shifts from one leg
to the other, easy-like as it replicates the rhythm.

Then there's a muted rhythm from the drums; as it
gradually intensifies, your knees start to move
and your hips follow.

You're getting into the groove—sort of
stand-dancing at your computer, thinking
onto the screen, when a trombone slips in with
a deep rhythmic vibe and your shoulders start
a slow shimmy.

Now your thoughts are in rhythm and your hands
on the keyboard can't keep up when a trumpet
starts to whine and wail; and oh man, then come
the saxophones, which always make you sweat:

First, the baritone begins with a low guttural growl,
then the alto starts to tease and taunt and finally,
the tenor joins in, slips in from the bottom with
a low growl then takes you to the top of the world
and damn! you're trying to get some work done,
but your hips are swaying, knees are bouncing,
shoulders are shaking, your head is rocking like a
bobblehead doll and your hands—your poor hands try
to stay on the keyboard but the music—the music lifts
them up and they move with it and can't type another
word.

****

THE WEB

As I sit here lonely in my room watching
        a little red spider
begin to spin its silken web I think back
        to a brighter time when
I was just a boy, each day filled with anticipation
        of the next time we would meet.
My young body quivered with elation
        at the thought.

We'd known each other since we were kids
        I watched you change and grow
from lanky little girl to goddess and you
        didn't even know how you warmed my heart
with every look and smile and deed
        or that if you had asked me for the moon
I would have happily agreed
        to capture it for you.

And the little red spider
keeps on spinning
one more thread from here
to there.

I remember now so clearly how
        I helped you on the day your car
broke down just before you went away
        to university far from home
and how tempted I was to say
        "This car will never run again
so I guess you'll have to stay and I
        will take you wherever you need to go."

You left and some months later
        I received a letter from you
saying you missed me and I'd better
        come to a homecoming dance.
You wanted to be with me and though
        it might seem strange
I would see we were meant
        to be together.

    And the little red spider
    keeps on spinning
    one more thread from here
    to there.

I sat there with that letter
        I just couldn't believe my eyes
and I set to packing two suitcases
        as it would be no surprise to me
if I wound up staying in that place
        you went to live.
I had no reason to stay here and in truth
        I'd readily give up everything to be with you.

I left my home to follow you
        and to show you I was the man
who could be all you'd ever need
        and you'd show me you can love
this backwoods boy who lived next door
        and was always there whenever
you wanted a little chat or needed a repair
        to whatever was amiss.

And the little red spider
keeps on spinning
one more thread from here
to there.

I arrived for that homecoming dance
        and we stayed ten years together
before the joy began to fade.
        And sometimes I would arrive home
Late to discover a man's coat, not mine
        and ask if you'd taken a lover.
You'd just smile and kiss me on the cheek.

Now life continues on that way,
        my love for you inside
so deep I can't bring myself to leave
        even though I've tried
And I watch that little red spider
        weaving threads from here to there
and I'm trapped in a web of homespun love
        and I can't get out of here.

******

FINDING RHYTHM

The young mother
totes her baby boy
in a canvas carrier
which hangs
from her shoulders
across her chest
The child faces forward
legs dangling

She moves purposefully
up the steep hill
in her attempt to reclaim
her pre-baby proportions
as the child makes sounds
which match the rhythm
of her steps

Ah-ah-ah-ah,
Ah-ah-ah-ah.

The child quiets
looks around
listens as if waiting
for inspiration
then begins again
more tentative with
a new, different vocal pattern
which continues for a few minutes

ah ah-ah (*//*)
ah ah-ah (*//*)

Again, he stops,
restless,
waves his arms
kicks his legs in agitation.
Minutes pass
and his voice,
slightly muted,
as if trying it out, sings:

ah-ah (*//*) (*//*)
ah-ah (*//*) (*//*)

His blue eyes open wide
he smiles
then, happily flails
those chubby arms and legs
and in a stronger voice continues

ah-ah (*//*) (*//*)
ah-ah (*//*) (*//*)

He keeps this up until the mother
reaches the top of the hill
completely unaware
that her child has found his rhythm
and he's running with it

****

I PROPOSE A TOAST

It is my observation that persistent
attention to the prickly ego-driven
politics which have pervaded
this country tends to pilfer one's
propensity for poetic, or in fact,
any expression of the intrinsic
beauty of time and place.

In an attempt to return to some
semblance of a more substantive reality,
it is important, and necessary, to divert
attention to more pleasant pastimes
such as, specifically, the creation,
or simply the enjoyment, of music.

"Music hath charm to soothe the savage beast,"
is an often-misquoted line from William
Congreve's play, "The Mourning Bride."
The actual line is: "Music hath charm
to soothe the savage breast," and though
that particular protuberance has been
known to soothe and relax and cause many
a man to sing its praises, it is the creators
of music, the composers, musicians, writers,
and singers, who offer the perfect diversion
from this pathetic preponderance of political
pollution, for what they give has the ability
to soothe and heal, move and transport,
distract and deflect.

Sit back, listen and even watch as the magic
of music fills the room. Feel the wave as it
springs forth from the stage. Let it wash,

scrub, cleanse, soothe, caress and penetrate
every pathway. Notice how it occupies
every recess, crack and crevice.

Absorb the potent power of the peace
it produces; then observe as it recedes
slowly and quietly, gently slides down
the walls, and flows across the floor
back to its place of origin, much
as the tide returns to the sea reclaiming
useless debris that sullies the sand.

So, it is with deepest gratitude,
that I propose a toast to those masterful,
imaginative, magnificent makers of music!

****

BALLET NATURALE

Shadows of branches
mix with sunlight
on the ground
as invisible breeze
creates music
to which they dance

Dark and light
mingle and separate
together apart
while above ground
limbs lift and sway
lissome arms
clothed in green leaves
and white petalled flowers
which they scatter
in appreciation of
the dancing shadows

I watch at my window
while a waltz plays
on the stereo and my arms
mimic the shadows
I prance around the room
swaying turning lost
in music and movement
until the last notes recede

Once more at the window
I stand and contemplate
the activity outside,
and become sadly aware
that the tree dances with
so much more grace than I

******

CONVERGENCE

In the early morning fog,
as cool mist rises from parched ground
after blazing heat of summer
I see you slowly move toward me.

Is it memory or imagination
that brings you to me now
as I sip coffee on the porch?
Music plays on a distant radio.

Your eyes meet mine as they did then
when for a moment my world stilled
and you stood before me, arm extended
and softly asked: "Shall we dance?"

Your hand reached for mine
like the hand of God on the ceiling
of the Sistine Chapel and suddenly
I knew I was born to be in your arms
and our dance was the creation of life.

In a silent explosion, only we could hear
we whirled around the floor
afloat in a green fluorescence
and converged in the electric air.

The music grows louder now, the song—
Did You Ever Really Love a Woman;
and you, who now know me so well,
reach out in this misty hush of morning
and ask, "Shall we dance?"

******

THE FIRST STEP

A young boy stands by the door
his back against the wall.
Uncomfortable in his suit and tie,
he watches wide-eyed.

They are colorful, he thinks,
even fascinating; but crowded together
like that—buzzing, limbs flailing,
teeth showing—it's frightening.

His apprehension grows.
He takes a deep breath
and tentatively, despite his terror,
he plunges in.

He slides slowly between
and around them. His hands
tremble and his heart thuds.
He takes care not to touch one.

Stunned by their communion
and incomprehensible bond,
he takes another breath
and finally reaches the far wall.

His father's voice in his head
tells him: *Choose one, any one.*
You can do this—just go for it:
    Ask a girl to dance.

******

CUBA - FIRST GLIMPSE

From the moment
the plane landed
we could feel it
all around us
in our heartbeats
in our footsteps
in the happy
smiling faces.

In a corner
of the airport
from a boombox
came some rhythms
almost primal
sizzling drumbeats—
Welcome travelers.
This is Cuba!

People stood up
started dancing
as if life had just begun.

They all danced
the Mambo
full of flair
and full of style.
And they sang out
with gusto as we
watched for a while.

As we drove through
Old Havana
centuries dissolved
as fairytale castles
with drawbridges,

filled our minds
with fantasies.

Stone fortresses
with cannons
sent visions
to our brains
of gallant knights
in shining armor
prepared to
save the day.

But fair maidens
crossed the draw-bridge;
There would be no war this day.

And they all danced
the Mambo
full of joy
and full of life;
and the soldiers
put their swords down
with no enemy in sight.

We rode on
through the city
in bright-colored cars
from years long gone;
their familiar
beauty and style
evoked teen dreams
we thrived upon.

On bumpy narrow
cobbled streets
we saw buildings
which amazed
in styles colonial,
Spanish and baroque
up through the
present day.

In our hotel lobby,
spicy rhythms
filled the night.

And we all danced
the Mambo
filled with passion
and delight,
and our hearts
beat to those rhythms
on that warm Havana night.

******

TANGO

I have always loved to dance—swing, Latin, ballroom. But Tango has never been part of my repertoire. Out of the blue, a friend invites me to Tango classes being offered by a dance teacher she knows, the first one to begin the following night. Long fascinated, though intimidated by the intensity and passion of this dance, I accept. I remember it as if it was yesterday:

The next evening, I arrive at the appointed address to find a large room with a glossy wooden dance floor surrounded by long tables and benches at which are seated several couples, a bunch of single ladies, and a decided absence of single men. The teacher has not yet arrived. Nonetheless, my friend, who is to be his assistant, proceeds to start the taped music.

Several men wander in, a few at a time, and find seats at the tables around the dance floor. A few minutes later I notice a man come through the doorway alone. He's not handsome in the traditional sense, but his long silver-gray hair tied in a ponytail low on his neck, in stark contrast to dark, leathery skin, is so striking, I find it difficult not to stare.

He's dressed in well-pressed dark blue cotton work clothes—obviously a man who does physical work. Not too tall, perhaps five foot nine or ten, and I suspect in his mid-fifties, he has a posture and demeanor that exude a continental confidence—and a body as solid as a tree trunk. As he walks, light reflects off a small gold hoop earring in his left earlobe; he's exotic as a gypsy right off a movie set.

I turn away to watch the few couples now dancing Tango and try to concentrate on their feet, how they move with the music and think it looks a bit complicated when all at once there's a hand held out in front of me, thick-fingered and strong, palm up, fingers together, and a deep voice, perhaps Russian accented says, "Come, we dance."

It's not a question; it's a statement. I look up into dark penetrating eyes, and see no hint of a smile on the deeply lined, rugged face, nor of challenge; it's completely neutral, waiting, as if there is no question as to what I will do. Struggling to pull my gaze from his, I stammer, "I don't know how."

"You come to dance," he says. Then, with a shrug, "So, we dance," and without another word he takes my hand and pulls me to my feet and into his arms, his thick right hand, so firm against the center of my back just above the waist, I'm fit to the curve of his body like the last piece of a jigsaw puzzle—chest to chest, waist to waist, thigh to thigh. His left hand holds my right at shoulder height, forearm to forearm all the way to the elbow.

The pulse of Tango is throbbing all around as his left thigh pushes against my right, forcing my right leg to slide back in the first step, then his right thigh against my left; left again, and then with quick pressure from his chest and hips, he moves me one step to the left, and forces my right foot to meet it and stop. Then the whole process again in the other direction: slow, slow, quick/quick, slow—T-A-NG-O.

I become hyper-aware of the beating of his heart and his deep, fast, rhythmic breathing, setting the pace for my own as we move: slow, slow, quick/quick, slow. Now his hands and body guiding my every move, he pulls me closer, every inch of our bodies touching as he rocks me forward into a lunge against him, then backward as he lunges against me. Then we straighten, twirl around, and step together, stop—T-A-NG-O. Around the dance floor we glide, melded together by the music and the heat of our bodies. We are the music on fire . . . THIS is tango!

The music stops just as we reach the table where we started. Like a throbbing, pulsing statue glued together at the core, we stand for a brief moment, then push away from one another, letting out our breath. He takes my hand, guides me to the bench, bows his head, and says: "Good"—then turns and walks away!

I am breathless! I reach for a pitcher of water and pour some into a cup. My hands are trembling. Hell, everything is trembling. What just happened? I've heard a thousand times Tango is passion, but DAMN!! I never imagined it was all this—I'm coming back! Oh, yeah!

I look around, but I don't see him again.

I continue going to the classes for the next month or so until the interested students dwindle to a bare handful and the teacher can no longer afford to rent the hall. I do learn to Tango somewhat with a few of the other men, but it never again feels like my first dance with that exotic man.

On the night of the last session, as I chat with a small group of people, the last dance is announced. Music fills the room, but I've already decided to slip out before it ends when I feel a heavy but gentle hand on my shoulder, hot breath on my neck, and a low, muffled, almost gruff voice in my ear: "Come. . .We dance."

******

surreptitiously
music captivates the soul
and moves it to dance

TANGO ARGENTINA

Buenos Aires - home of the Tango;
on every street a reminder.
I watched dancers come together
on cardboard dancefloors in the street,
in colorful extravaganzas on the stage,
in the darkness of neighborhood milongas.

So simple at first: a couple begins to dance.
As the music progresses, the dance
becomes an emotion, a state of being,
an organic transformation that fuses body
and mind, movement and music.

Now, Buenos Aires behind me, I still feel
the sensations, hear the incantations
from every window and doorway,
the orchestrations, vibrations,
the palpable magic that creates a
unique passion which defies description.

It follows me down the street, infuses
my blood, silently whispers to my soul:

    "Feel my pulse.
    I am your heart.
    I am Tango.
    Feel me and dance."

And suddenly, I am dancing—
on the street, in the woods,
on the sand, in the clouds.

I am air and rhythm and flowing grace.
I'm the fire of desire, the joy, the pain,
the fragility and ferocity of life.

    "Feel my pulse.
    I am your heart.
    I am Tango."

****

PEOPLE

THE ARTIST

He wasn't a so-called "modern" artist, not abstract or impressionist or any of the other art forms of which I know little. His was a kind of "rampant realism," "imaginary movement" or "not so still life" if one can envision such an art form.

When I was a child, I watched him for hours as I stood unnoticed in dappled sunlight among shadows of trees at the window of his studio, a run-down shack in the woods, as he began a new painting.

I had heard his name was Jacques.

Always dressed in the same wrinkled, long-sleeved, paint-splotched red shirt and baggy black pants, which he continually tugged at with his left hand as they slid down over his big belly, Jacques confronted the large blank canvas propped on his easel.

He always seemed to have an angry scowl on his unshaven face when he began a new painting. He splashed a wad of thick oil paint, usually a beige or tan color, onto the canvas with almost startling force; then stood squarely in front of it and just stared as if by doing so it would suddenly spring to life.

With a palette knife in his right hand, he sloshed the paint around into a free-form shape, not quite round or oval, square or oblong. He moved like a madman. His arms waved back and forth, thick strands of his long black hair whipped his face as he smeared colors onto/into the shape: a dot of red in the center, a smudge of black in a corner, then blue, yellow, green—on the red, on the black, seemingly at random, repeatedly hitching up his pants with his free hand.

My young eyes still saw nothing recognizable on the canvas during those frenzied hours of creation, so mesmerized was I by his frantic yet complete immersion in what he was doing until finally, he stepped back and again stood squarely in front of his easel, head cocked to one side, contemplative.

Abruptly, he picked up a small, thin stylus from the mass of paint tubes and odd-sized implements and brushes on the table beside the easel and, with an uncharacteristic, graceful flourish, signed, or rather, engraved his name into the thick paint in the lower right-hand corner of the canvas.

Afterward, he moved to the side, half-turned, and bowed to an invisible audience as if he had been watched during the entire insane period of creation of what then unbelievably, was a perfect portrait of a familiar face of a celebrity or politician, a random person, or a child or animal with a lively sparkle in the eyes that made me laugh, or a tear I was sure I actually saw roll down the cheek; flowers and trees that seemed to sway in an invisible breeze, or a dog running down a street, saliva dripping over the bone held in its mouth.

I'd watched him do this on several occasions, each time astounded by the result of his precision. But there was one time, the very last time, as he stepped away from the canvas, the figure in the painting stared back at me, a perfect mirror of my current disbelief, so clearly reflected on the canvas, it was chilling. How could he have captured what was not present until that moment when he didn't even know I was there?

Or did he?

****

LEGACY

It began as a blob of clay,
worked by the hands of an artist
who could not or would not
allow herself to create art
which might garner more
attention than she herself.

She had little patience
for demanding detail work.
She cursed and babbled
to herself while she worked,
discredited and abused
her creation in invisible ways.

Frustrated by her inability
to bend it to her will
she assigned it to others
to smooth and finesse
until finally, after years,
she deemed it "done."

Although quite unfinished
many found this work
uniquely attractive, were
amused by its imperfections,
captivated by its clumsiness
and ultimately grew to love
and admire it as a true work of art.

Over time it took on a life
and personality of its own,
while the artist, initially hailed
as a genius, was soon forgotten

in the shadow of her masterwork
bringing her greatest fear to fruition.

Her art would be remembered
long after her name was forgotten.

****

SOME PEOPLE

In quiet moments late at night
my mind sometimes wanders
to encounters with people
I've cared for and loved
who have moved far away
or have passed on and I long
for their presence.

I'm reminded of how smooth or
arduous those encounters
may have been—some pure joy,
others, a constant challenge;
and now in my mind, their best
is more visible than ever it was.

Memories hover in the air,
then settle in colorful piles
like autumn leaves—pieces of life
whose seasons have passed,
and I want to inhale their essence,
roll around in them, to again feel
their warmth to fill the space
they left in my heart.

Faces, places, scenes from a lifetime
are fit together by recollections
of what once was or might have been
and though some were so easy
and others not so, during moments
of contemplation, absent the chaos
of their presence, there arises
an irrefutable revelation of abiding love.

And I miss them all.

****

MARGIE

Margie and I have exchanged "Hi, how are you's" for years as we pass one another on the street.

One day, an ambulance and two firetrucks, sirens screaming, lights flashing, raced up the hill to where Margie lived, though I don't know in precisely which house.

It seems everyone in the area knows Margie just a little. Snippets of her life have circulated like a game of telephone. She's ninety-two years old, played tennis until recently, and had been a dancer on Broadway, where she met her husband, a fellow hoofer. She was widowed ten years ago and has lived alone ever since.

Margie walks miles each day in the neighborhood and knows more people around this area than I ever will, even though I've lived here for forty years; she climbs up and down that steep hill with apparent ease.

She's so thin and frail, I've often thought, with concern for this woman I hardly know.

I continued on my way to do my necessary chores, marketing, getting keys made, etc., and a few hours later, as I approached the corner near my home, there was Margie, walking with her jaunty, graceful step up the street toward the hill.

"Margie," I called. She turned.

"I saw an ambulance and firetrucks on your hill earlier. I was worried about you."

"Oh, I'm fine." I've been walking—you know, before the rain. But I hope my neighbor is ok—he has a bad heart.

He's old—doesn't get out much. I guess I'd better keep moving," she said with an impish grin; then she did a little Chicago shuffle and sauntered on her way. After a few steps, she turned back and waved:

"Good to see you," we said in unison.

I watched her glide away and thought: *She must have been one hell of a dancer.*

******

NORMA

In a restless dream I heard a sound
        a piercing mournful cry
of such deep despair and pathos
        yet so childlike that I
forced myself to wakefulness
        rubbed my eyes, and then
as I wondered if it was just a dream
        I heard the sound again.

A shiver rippled through me
        and as my feet reached for the floor
a vague familiarity stirred
        I'd heard that sound before.
The air grew still in my darkened room.
        I could see nothing at all
when suddenly a cloud appeared
        at the far end of the hall.

It was big and gray and ominous
        yet had shimmery moonlit glow
and as it glided toward my bedroom door
        I gathered things to throw.
I sat tense upon my bed in wait
        my weapons piled high
not knowing if I'd need to fight
        but if I did, I'd try.

It floated through the doorway
        and stopped at the foot of my bed
where it slowly began to dissipate
        and left there in its stead
stood Norma in full uniform
        quite whole, I couldn't believe.
A purple heart graced her lapel
        three stripes upon her sleeve.

It had been some time, six months
        or more, since I had seen her last
and I sensed she'd come to me this night
        to let me know she'd passed.
We'd met several years before when
        I worked in the Veterans' Hall.
A bent and shriveled white-haired crone
        she hardly spoke at all.

She'd been a prisoner of war
        in Korea I'd heard it said.
No kin or friends came by these days
        or knew if she was alive or dead.
So once a week I visited.
        I'd say: "Norma, you know I'm here
and if you'd like my company
        just offer me a chair."

She spat and flailed or simply stared
        and cried her mournful cry
and no recognition lit her face
        as months and years went by.
Then one day when I went to visit
        she looked up with a frown.
She scowled at me and waived her arms
        and then she yelled, "sit down."

She didn't say another word
        but we sat 'til it was late
and when next I went to visit
        she'd been transferred out of state.
Now here she was before me
        with life glowing in her eyes.
Her lips turned up in laughter
        as she noticed my surprise.

I hope she's in a better place
        maybe happy in her hometown.
But Norma if you need company—
        I'm here. Have a chair . . . sit down.

****

LEAVING NEW ORLEANS

I

My whole life's been here in the Big Easy;
done some drinkin', a bit of druggin',
some of what they call "general debauchin'"
and got me lots of good lovin' and huggin'.

You should go on down to St. Charles
because far as you can see, strings of beads
dangle like vines from the trees.
Those Mardi Gras gals flash their wares
just to score some of these.

And there's a guy down on Bourbon Street,
who makes love to the keys—
and man, his music's got the power
to bring you clear to your knees.

His friend makes notes full of passion
float out of his horn,
so mournful yet joyful,
you'll bless the day you were born.

These streets are filled with color—
beads, clothing, faces;
the wealthy and not so
from all races and places.

There are drunk folks and sober
musicians, magicians,
and folks damn near naked—
ain't got no inhibitions;

There's grannies and trannies,
barkers and mimes,
and down on their luck folks
beggin' for dimes.

Young world-weary women
in doorways entice–in their fashion.
There's so much life in these streets
and the neons keep flashin'.

It's easy to lose yourself
in this hypnotic abyss
but a big ship waits for me
on the shores of the Miss.

II

As I leave, all sounds fade;
the world's grayer and colder
And me? Well, I've got more weight
than my bags on my shoulder

I'm memorizin' these streets,
makin' my way real slow.
Man, I'm leavin' the "Easy" life,
the only world I know.

Goodbye "liquid sunshine"—
what we call a rainy spell.
And when I die, I'll be movin'
to the "underground hotel."

My kids bought me a fancy cruise
they call "the trip of my dreams,"
but there is no better place for me
than right here in New Orleans.

I look around one last time
and feel hot tears on my face;
I'll hold what I see here in
a kind of mental embrace.

My rhythms are changing',
the old clock's windin' down.
Truth is: if it stops
I hope it's here in this town.

Oh, I guess I'm bein' foolish;
could be good to get away.
If I can just convince myself—
c'mon Lord—help me pray.

That muddy old river's
splashin' hard on the pier.
And that fancy white ship
is like a ghost sittin' there.

I trudge up the gangplank,
my beat-up bags in tow.
Too late to turn back now,
so I guess I'm good to go.

I watch my Crescent City
slowly float away
but Lord willin', somehow
I'll get back here one day.

******

LOCKER ROOM TALK

While the rest of the world
is threatening to implode
the ladies in the locker room
in from their daily swim
strip naked and stand
in open shower stalls
comfortable in the company
of friendly strangers who
congregate weekdays
in the locker room post-swim
to chat and exchange ideas
as they shampoo and soap
and luxuriate in the luminous
energy they encounter.

Exhilarated and relaxed,
emancipated from physical
and mental inhibition, they
revel in pure and complete
nakedness regardless of size,
shape, age, ethnicity, or
financial status.

A voice rings out:
"Does anyone know how to
get rubber bands out of wet hair?"
"Oh, sure," comes a response
"I'll help you with that.
What stall are you in?"

"Hey," says another, "does anyone
have any experience with gout?
My husband is suffering like crazy."
Another voice: "Oh, I do;
my husband suffers from it too;

I have lots of information . . . I'll
bring it for you."

It goes on and on, day after day --
the caring, the sharing, the
reaching out, the responding.
Old school. Golden Rule.

The ladies in the locker room get
naked, ask for what they need,
give what they can, then go back
to their separate lives while
the rest of the world threatens
to implode because everyone
wants to take and no one wants to give.

****

DO THEY NOTICE

They flit in and out
of an ornate glass castle
with skill and agility.
Light creates kaleidoscopic
colors and designs
in their watery home
as they cavort without care—
children playing hide and seek
in a garden of rocks
and swaying greenery.

There is such peace
in their turquoise world
protected as they are
by the ever-watchful eyes
of a lone diver whose air tank
keeps their world pristine
and of a tiny mermaid
who waves and blows kisses
her long hair swaying as they pass.

What must they think
if they think
or feel if they feel
these carefree creatures
who do not breathe
the bitter and polluted air
of the chaotic outside world?

Do they notice
who sprinkles sustenance
like manna from heaven
over their world each day?

Do they notice me as I watch
them play or suspect I dream
I am the mermaid whose kisses
will forever bubble to the surface?

****

WALLS & DOORS

Beware the walls we build
     to block our way
Note doors that divide
     outside from in
Tame shadowed thoughts
     that keep dreams at bay
Lest we lose
     what we should win

The path is clear
     for those who seek
with open heart—
     not hard to find
The walls will crumble
     with words we speak
and open new doors
     in our minds

****

WHAT IF

What if I dared to stand
before the world
to bare my naked soul
with no mask, nor wall
nor weapon to protect me.

      What then?

And what if I, trembling
at the prospect of scrutiny
and judgment, wanting to flee,
stood anyway,
eye to curious eye.

      What then?

And what if, perchance,
the world were to see
not the me I see
but one so unique and true
it asked for more.

      What then?

******

CLOSET CINDERELLA

She was a strong and independent girl
educated, intelligent, fun.
Heads would turn each time she'd pass
and she knew how to get things done.

Men would swarm around her
captivated by her charms
and she would give them all a chance
but not stay in one man's arms.

Oh, she'd had romantic rendezvous
with men from near and far
but hadn't found her special one
that elusive unreachable star.

Yet in her secret heart of hearts
though no one would conceive it
She dreamed of a prince, a gallant knight—
even she couldn't quite believe it.

She fantasized being swept away
in a storybook romance
and wondered if it came to be
would she dare to take the chance?

> She was a closet Cinderella,
> hiding in plain sight.
> No one in the world would guess
> she yearned for Mr. Right.

Then, along came a goofy
brainiac guy talking his nerdy talk.
He made her laugh at herself, and at him
the first time they went for a walk.

Unwittingly he taught her things
she'd never learn from a book—
how to live real life and love real love
and enjoy the work it took.

She smiled a lot as days went by;
her workload felt much lighter
and when she walked the avenue
the sun seemed to shine brighter.

She started singing all the time
in her crazy off-key way—
outside the shower, for heavens' sake,
and it was perfectly okay.

But late at night when all was still
from somewhere deep inside
sprang a fear of losing herself in him
and the child inside her cried.

    She was a closet Cinderella;
    now she couldn't sleep at night.
    She was afraid this nerdy fella
    might just be her gallant knight.

Time went by and day by day
she opened up her heart,
expecting that inner child to cry
but it didn't ever start.

She tried hard not to notice that
holding his hand caused sensations
far more intimate to her
than her more "intimate" relations.

Then one day it happened
and from his lips she heard
the question to which her answer
might invoke the dreaded "C" word—
Commitment!

Waves of panic engulfed her
from her head down to her toes
A "yes" would mean getting naked
and wouldn't involve removing clothes.

She wracked her brain for what to do
then took a long deep breath
And loud and clear she answered with
an ardent elated "YES"!

> She'd been a closet Cinderella
> Now she just might have it all.
> She'll be strutting down the aisle
> because she's going to the ball!

****

LOVE & LOSS

NOW AND ZEN

You are part of me
You became so the moment we met
and I became a part of you.

If each becomes part of the other
How many does it take to create one?
The answer is: we are together one,
each a work incomplete
finished only when we no longer
grow from one another
each of us the sum of all parts
the product of every communion.

There is a piece of you in me
As I honor myself, I honor you
because we are one.

When you leave this plane of being
you will be complete and beautiful
and the part of you in me will go on.

****

THE AFFECTION CONNECTION

There are people without motive
who might catch one unaware
whose smile or simple handshake
says "I'm so glad you're here"

Perhaps they think you're funny
maybe quirky, sweet or kind
Or just have a certain something
not easily defined

They may sense some inner frailty
vulnerability at your core
which puts them in protective mode
to keep vipers from your door

Affection has no gender
It's organically inspired
It is the purest form of caring
the most precious and desired

A confection of unique sweetness
with no dietary restriction
it requires cautious consumption
lest it lead one to addiction
But no finer salve to soothe the soul
in moments of pain or dejection
exists among either man or beast
than an authentic affection connection.

******

I LOVE

From a thick carpet of new grass
I watch clouds float in the blue sky
a light breeze tickles my face
        in a gentle caress

Scent of earth and clover beneath me
sweet jasmine and crepe myrtle above
I delight in the miracle of simply being.
        I sleep.

A spectral white dove ascends from my breast
soaring into the magnificent infinite sky
through cushions of white clouds that
        morph pink and lilac in the west.

She flies east into the plush black velvet night
studded with diamonds blinking a silent
message to this mystical beacon of peace.
        She sings joyfully

as once more she enters the orange glow
of morning and descends back to the heart
her place of origin. The sun smiles in welcome
        as she returns home.

On a zephyr, wispy white feathers
brush my face in a gentle awakening.
Squinting against the light I rise.
I am here, now, and today—
        I love.

✳✳✳✳✳✳✳

WHAT WAS THAT?

What was that when
he took my hand to say hello
the handsome stranger
on a crowded avenue
whose eyes were tunnels
into a future just beyond
the scope of my vision
hypnotically inviting me
daring me to enter . . .
at my own risk!

And when a bolt of lightning
shot from his palm into mine
so that I jumped back
but only far enough that my hand
stayed solidly in his, the effervescent
tingle of electricity ignited
my unsuspecting soul.

And the sensuous smolder
of his voice threatened
to consume me and sent
shivers of pleasure and promise
through my veins, as my heart
suddenly slowed to reason
and warned, "WAIT"!

What was that?

And later as I recorded those
surreal moments in hurried script
lest memory abandon me
I felt his presence on the page
infusing the space between each line.

And with every breath I inhaled
the mesmeric heat and musk of him
and heard my own voice caution
that the seducer and the seduced
are indistinguishable, a notion which
at once excited, exhilarated, and terrified
yet assured we would meet again
he and I on some crowded avenue.

And with each chance encounter
by the transcendent power of mutual
anticipation I was transported through
tunnel after tunnel all the way to now.

And still I can feel in the air the promise,
the electricity, the tingle, and I need not ask

    What was that?

****

my lips still recall
the gentle sweetness of yours
a lifetime ago

I REMEMBER

Here you are before me after so many years.
You smile the familiar smile
that filled my days with sunlight.

Oh, how long it has been since merely
one's presence filled me so completely
made me more, more . . . everything.

I have yearned to feel that way again
to count the moments 'til we would meet
to breathe your essence in the air.

I look at your face and remember
fingertips on flushed cheeks,
soft lips on open palms

A love so improbable, impossible;
differences insurmountable
though the love never lied.

We parted heart in heart forever.

I love you still for that sacred memory
not sure if you were what I remember
or only what I wanted you to be.

Now in your eyes I see that question reflected
and know it was real if only for a moment.
Oh yes, I remember and I search . . .
for nothing less will suffice.

******

A FACE IN THE CROWD

A face in a passing crowd
captures my consciousness
transports me back in time
to the tenderness of a special love

Carefree days, quiet nights,
the first fleeting taste of his lips
Oh, how merely the thought of him
makes me swell with desire.

I come alive at the sound of his voice
the sweet smile, for me alone
that assures my heart there is no other.
His touch renews me; the years fall away.

Funny how memory fills a faded dream
with such glorious new color—
as one might restore a precious work of art
with more vibrance than ever it had.

Would I know him I wonder
if he stood before me now.
Would his eyes light with recognition of me?
The mind sometimes forgets, not so, the heart.

A face in a passing crowd
reminds me of a special love.

I can't remember his name.

****

THE STOLEN HOURS

The sun is buried in thick layers
of gray the only hint of its presence
an iridescent smudge in the clouds
which casts an eerie spotlight
on the flowering treetop
outside my window.

White petals like snowflakes
float on the wind, lend haunting
beauty to the translucent mist.
His familiar face appears
from deep in the haze, untouchable
as a dream one tries to hold onto
in the ascent to wakefulness.

Words and thoughts spring
from the depths of consciousness
to fill and surround like the very
cells of my body as I remember
stolen hours, furtive encounters,
surreptitiously snatched
from the rushing river of time
each a healing respite from
the rigors of real life, times we shared
our truest selves free of public masks.

Innocent but secret, treasured minutes
ticked away like lifegiving heartbeats
as together we laughed, cried, talked,
and healed and after, returned renewed
to our daily worlds.

Outside the window the sky brightens.
Sunlight breaks through clouds.
Patches of blue appear.

What had I been thinking—
something about a river.
and there was a sense
that a fire was starting.

****

LIKE DAVID

I want a hard-bodied man
like the one who emerged
from the ocean that day at the beach,
whose tall lithe body
was perfectly sculpted
with every toned and sinuous
muscle rippling as he walked

He stopped near a dark blue blanket
a few yards down the beach,
retrieved a towel and proceeded
to vigorously rub his body dry
then his hair and with bare hands
smoothed it back allowing
one dark curl to escape and fall
onto his brow

Now as a more "mature" woman
I like my men a little softer and cuddlier
definitely bigger than me with some
but not too much squeezable stuff
to hold on to.

But still, I wanted to take this one home—
not for some bawdy rapacious romp—no
but as a piece of art to display in my home,
unclad for all to see, like a replica
of Michelangelo's David.

I would place him in the living room,
drape a velvet scarf on his shoulder
and use it to . . .dust him, maybe daily—
run it gently over every smooth and not
so smooth inch of him from head to toe.

After all, it's important to take
good care of objects of art.
******

WALK WITH ME BY THE WATER

Walk with me by the water,
put your hand in mine.
Let our fingers intertwine.
Watch our reflections
float along the bay
while our shadows follow
and cling to us like the past
which never really leaves
but fades into darkness
until awakened by a new day.

Ripples in the water alter
the details of our reflected faces
much as passing years
etch deep crevices and lines of life
to protect and preserve
precious remnants of youth
left beneath which no measure
of time can erase.

So, walk with me by the water
with your hand in mine,
our fingers intertwined.
We will lead our shadows
to bright tomorrows
and leave the past behind;
and if age reclaims our memories,
our youth will come out to play
and I will hold your hand in mine
until time slips it away.

****

ON THE EDGE

There are things that hover
on the edge of your vision
like a halo you don't notice until
you stop whatever it is you're doing:

perhaps a picture . . . a scene recalled
from the warmth of childhood which
has lingered unnoticed in the littlest
corner of your consciousness,

possibly a piece of music which
surreptitiously insinuated itself
into your DNA long ago and emerges
unsummoned like a sigh,

a fragrance that floats on the fringe
of reality its origin a mystery
yet its sweetness evokes scenarios
from a long-ago time or place

or the person forever poised
on the periphery of every
waking moment whose presence
warms the spirit simply by being there.

All fan the flames of imagination
for fantasy cannot be forbidden;
almost close enough to touch
but elusive as a dream.

****

NOT NOW

What dark and stormy clouds
come stealthy on the unsuspecting dawn
to invade this day when seasons
of yesterdays were bright
with the joyful light and warmth of love
which protected innocent flowers
ere cold winds and grating sands
destroyed with seeds of doubt.

Oh, fool that was a neophyte
 in this harsh world ever trusting
the false and fickle light
now grown dark and cold.

The heart beats oddly in this new climate.

Oh, search for one small shaft of light
to part the clouds and force the sun
to warm again. Search for a gentle breeze
to float upon in this altered world
'til this restive heart may once again
confide in light and open to its seductive sway
in some elusive distant hour . . .
but not now, not this day.

******

GONE

Overnight it can change
you awaken one morning
and something is gone—
those feelings deep inside
that held you hostage for so long

Gone are the words which like whips
seemed to shape your destiny—
the false promises, retractable love;
but no longer are you the one who mourns

Sometimes you see glimpses
of a happier more joyful time,
another life, the one meant to be,
should have been

You conjure words you've heard
in places you cannot recall
and wonder whose they were;
not yours. Were they his?

Suddenly one day it's all gone—
the words, the promises, the damage
that lingered for years after he left
and you're free and whole

But oddly, you still miss . . .
you miss the rainbow—
that illusion of something beautiful
that never really was.

******

THOSE WORDS

One night in your sleep you said "I love you"
I know now you always did—love me
But I wanted, needed to hear you
        say them out loud—those words

I thought back then I saw it in your eyes,
your smile, felt it in your touch;
but still, I needed, wanted, to hear you
        say them out loud—those words

You were afraid and wouldn't, couldn't;
"Just words," you said, "overused, meaningless."
But, oh, how I wanted, needed, to hear you
        say them—out loud

I waited so long, patient and hopeful.
The words never came, those words,
that I needed, wanted, to hear you
        say—out loud

Time passed; life went on and I found
someone who understood about
those words, someone who also
        wanted and needed to hear them

A day came when you took my hand in yours;
your face was soft, your eyes shiny with tears
and you said them out loud—those words
        I had so wanted, needed to hear you say.

        But it was too late.

****

THEN AND NOW

An old photograph
reminds me of you
and the long-ago night
when your sweet lips
first touched mine
and my world changed orbit

So much time has passed
Seasons have altered the landscape
as time has changed you
The colors of both have faded
My world still turns but slower

As I did back then
I come alive with you near
Your touch renews me
The air is filled with wonder
Let's make love and then please leave

****

CLOSING THE DOOR

Years have passed.
The phone rings
displays a number
deleted from my thoughts.
I let the machine answer
but listen to the message.

Suddenly I hear you speaking
as if time has magically healed
the wounds of yesterday.
You don't understand—
there is no longer room
for you in my life.

I wonder at those who mourn
what once was when the past
held only heartbreak and pain.
It was not difficult to move on
to simply erase my error.

Now you try to slip through
a crack in that closed door.
I don't know who you are.
I thought I did but I was wrong.
You were simply a figment
of imagination, created in my mind.

Where did I put that damned eraser?

******

ONE FOR THE ROAD

Maybe it was coffee he ordered instead of another scotch when last call was announced at the dive bar he wound up in that night—because coffee always gave him a good start in the morning, the way it slid down his throat in a silken wave; and what the hell, it was morning—3:00 a.m.

But this sludge went down like alcohol on an open wound. No matter. It was sufficient to sober him up enough to get home safely, which was the point, though another scotch might chase away the memory.

Damn, he really had a thing for that gal; no woman had ever stopped him cold the way she did. They'd been out dancing and he loved the way her body felt against his, loved the way she made him laugh and how he started to feel empty when she wasn't around.

They'd gone out on the terrace and kissed—necked like a couple of horny teenagers then wound up in a room on the fourteenth floor of that hotel and made beautiful love for hours. He had never felt the way he did with her, never made love like that—like it was his last time and he wanted it to go on forever. He loved the smell of her skin, especially when she was hot with passion and he got chills when he ran his hands over the curve of her hips. She was magic, made him feel like he was the only man in the world and oh, the things she did with her tongue on his body; and her hands—where did she learn to touch a man like that?

But when he tried to tell her how he felt she stopped him cold and geez, he was usually the one who said stuff like that. What was it she said? Oh yeah:

"A kiss is just a kiss, and sex is just sex.
Passion is good for your health but it's not
a promise."

And then, "It's late and I need to get home."

Too stunned to do anything else, he'd taken her home and then wound up in this dive bar. He called out to the bartender:

"Give me another cup of this sludge . . .
and throw a shot of scotch in it . . . one
for the road."

****

WHEN IDOLS FALL

Most everyone has had one
at some time in life, perhaps
a favorite performer or teacher,
a friend or lover who basked
in the light of your veneration
from atop the golden pedestal
you so generously provided
for your daily worship.

But that was before all illusions
were suddenly shattered
by slow revelation of the
undesirable facets festering
beneath the glowing exterior
displayed to the world.

Each such loss spawns a rumbling
thunder so deep in your core
it echoes in your heart for days,
weeks, or even years; if finally, it
quiets, the lingering void is dark,
deep and aches to be filled

A desperate quest begins, and
too often, history repeats;
no lessons learned.

The hamster wheel continues to turn
for the heart, for the world—
      when idols fall.

****

PRECIOUS THINGS

I've never been one to collect stuff
or get attached to things
like china, crystal giftware,
art, or jewelry fit for kings

But there are items I hold dear,
the reason, odd for some to see,
since whatever value they may have
is visible only to me:

A stone gargoyle on the mantle,
my brother gave to me;
a hot dog vendor music box
from a New York friend, you see.
A ring given to me by my son,
a bracelet from my daughter
a carafe from a friend for my bedside stand
if in the night I need some water

Such things are precious to my heart
from folks I love so dearly;
some I'll never see again,
some only once or twice yearly.
But each item makes me think of them
however far they stray
and the memory of their giving
keeps them with me every day

****

ODE TO A TREE
(For my father)

The tree was a constant presence
for as long as I can remember,
so much a part of my life
though I barely noticed it back then.

Its branches reached out to shelter,
reassure, protect; I saw it survive
stunning storms and silently,
it taught me strength, endurance.

Frightened, sad or lonely
I sat in the cool calm shelter of its shadow
and it comforted me, and others.
All left it behind.

When time came for me to leave,
without a thought I did,
secure in the knowledge the tree
would be there as always.

Was it a sudden lightning strike
or simply the ravages of time
that one day split it down the center
revealing its broken heart?

And still, it stood, severed in two,
half broken and shriveled, half alive
and strong but lost and out of place
in an unfamiliar forest.

Might I have saved it had I stayed?
Now it withers, day by day,
and I am powerless to return
the gifts it gave, too late realized.

What will my world be without this tree,
its silent wisdom? I pray one day
I will be honored in memory as the
enduring tree of someone's childhood.

******

THE HOUSE

They arrive together, the sisters,
at the old family house,
not a home, really.
It was never that.

Vacant now for years, it shows
evidence of four-legged intruders,
in drawers, on tattered cushions
and frayed carpets.

Absent from consciousness for even longer,
their dread of emptying the place overwhelms.
Memories swept away in the tide of time
return in a flood of brackish waves.

They climb the stairs to the upper floor.
Wordlessly, they pull garments from drawers,
closets, cram them into donation bags—dresses,
shoes, belts, handbags and hats, suits and coats;
and gifts they'd given with the best of intentions,
still wrapped, stuffed into dark corners.

Then, one finds her own wedding dress,
promised to have been preserved;
but, no, it is stained and ruined,
sadly, like the marriage it had defined.
The sisters' eyes meet briefly.
They hurriedly bury it in a bag.

From room to room they roam,
clearing clutter, discarding debris,
fascinated that the only trace of
them that remains, are the large
portraits which hang in the living room.

Painted by mother, as much a tribute
to her own artistry as to her children,
the two sisters and their younger brother
hang dust-covered and staring.

After hours of "cleansing" the upstairs
of everything to be donated or trashed,
they drag the bags down the stairs
and into the garage, then go outside
into the cool fresh air and sunshine.

And then come the red birds—not
cardinals or robins but tiny birds,
so red as to be cartoonish.
They land in the grass and sing.

They sing as if their little hearts will burst
and as the sun begins to set, they fly away
in one brilliant wave of red.

****

SOMETIMES A LIGHT
(For my friend)

Sometimes a light, the likes of which
one rarely encounters
appears in the dark of a place
its shine so bright one may back away
later to realize this light
whispers welcome
with a near familial flicker.

Sometimes a light creates joy
with the smallest snippet of its power
and when fully illuminated
the warmth of its glow brightens
everything around it and accentuates
all the best parts.

Sometimes a light emanates
from a spirit so incandescent
its presence and makes everyone
feel more important and more loved
than they ever believed possible.

Sometimes a light even when
extinguished, continues to shine
in everything and everyone who
was blessed to bask in its glow.

Sometimes a light.

******

TO BE REMEMBERED

To be remembered with love
is the greatest gift for both
those who have passed on
and those left behind

To be remembered as a light
in times of darkness
and as a loving touch
in times of loneliness

To be remembered for wisdom
in times of doubt
and for rejoicing
in times of glory

To be remembered for caring
in times of illness
and joyfulness
in times of celebration

To be remembered for artistry
yet also for humility
and for accomplishment
but always for humanity
To be remembered for all this
is to live and be remembered
in hearts and minds for always.

****

THE PLACES WE GO
(For my brother)

"I'm glad you're here," he said, squeezing my hand. He'd said those same words to me each of the many times I had traveled across the country to visit him, coupled with "speak to me" meaning I should tell him what has been going on in my life and again, during the last crisis six months ago when I had raced across the world to where he was now living.

This time I had arrived in the morning with a hastily packed suitcase and no sleep, in time to hear him say those words to me for the last time. I bid him a devastated tearful goodbye the next day but stayed some weeks in the place he had lived to feel his presence in the people and things that defined him.

Life has not been the same since my return; I have not been the same. Peace eludes me.

Now, I sit at my dining room table, curtains drawn, creating near darkness, and light a scented candle—Sea Breeze, it's called. I flop back in my chair in the way that always infuriated my mother, my bottom on the edge of the seat, legs stretched out in front of me, shoulders slouching against the chair back, and stare at the yellow flame. I take a deep breath, hold it as long as possible, exhale slowly, and repeat again and again.

The tension begins to recede, my shoulders relax as my eyes close to slits, open only enough to receive the golden beam emanating from the candle's flame. It sheds warm light on the frenzied activity in my brain. I inhale deeply, taking the golden beam in further; I hold it, bask in it, as it slowly warms and saturates my nasal passages, brain, throat, arms, chest, abdomen, inching its way down to my toes. My eyes close, as with each succeeding breath, I absorb more golden light until I am glowing with its power.

My eyes open in a place where gentle waters ripple over ancient rocks, an azure sea spread out before me toward an unreachable horizon. Its banks overflow with brilliantly hued wildflowers. As I sit cross-legged on a thick carpet of soft green grass, butterflies flutter past my face so close they are reminiscent of a child's eyelash kisses; they fill me with joy. A soft breeze ruffles my hair as the sun caresses my bare skin.

I stand and walk to the water's edge, climb into a bright red kayak I find nestled between the rocks, push away from shore, and begin to paddle toward the horizon.

I glide through the blue water, entranced by the glitter of the sun's reflection dancing on its surface and lose track of time; when I look around, the shoreline has disappeared.

Tension pulls at my limbs and despite the warm sun and the intensity of my paddling, a chill creeps through me. I continue paddling and soon before me, a tiny island appears—flower-laden, green and lush. A gigantic weeping willow tree stands regally in the center; its leaves sway in the light sea breeze like a flowing green gown.

I guide the kayak to the shore, wedge it between two rocks, and climb out. I am still trembling as I approach the tree and sit down with my back against her trunk, her long tresses rendering me invisible to the world. I begin to relax as the gentle slap of the water on the rocks, the breeze whispering through the swaying leaves, and the buzzing of a bee create a magical choir that sweetly sings: "I'm glad you're here."

A large bumblebee buzzes past my face and back again, and again. I tense once more, gripped by a childhood fear, and squeeze my eyes closed as the bee continues its pattern buzzing back and forth so close I can almost feel its wings, and, in the buzzing, I hear what sounds like "speak to me."

My eyes pop open and I watch the bee, its flight pattern getting shorter so it's almost hovering in front of my face, buzzing louder. "Speak to me," buzzes the bee. I shake my head as total confusion numbs my senses and slowly, as if in a trance, I begin to speak my heart—my joy, my fears, my pain my tears. The bee has landed and sits quietly on my shoulder no longer buzzing, my silent voice pouring forth all that lies within me in a telepathic communion between the bee, the tree, the sea, and me.

Sometime later, my vision clears as if I've awakened from a deep sleep, and cognition pushes its way through the magical mist. I stand and make my way back to the kayak. I feel lighter than air, and as I begin to paddle away from the island, I feel a sharp sting on my left shoulder. My hand comes up to touch it, just as a large bumblebee flies past my face once, twice, and away; instinctively, I reach out and call after it: "I love you."

******

I FEEL YOU

In the bright of morning
sun hot on my face you appear
a momentary vision
which warms me even more
and I feel you

I feel you in the intake of breath
at that sudden imagined
appearance and in the shock
of disappointment at my error
and

I feel you as birds perceive
the endless sky which allows
their freedom to fly at will
without question or judgment
and

I feel you as leaves respond
to a whisper of breeze
that makes them flutter and dance
and as the wind makes them sing
and

I feel you in the songs you loved
in the many gifts you gave
the books you treasured
the poems that made you smile
and

I feel you the way I feel music
how it penetrates the thickest psychic walls
to create a peace that calms the spirit
and soothes the soul
and

I feel you when sleep is near
and behind closed eyes
I see you clearly
and you live.

You live . . . in me . . .
and I feel you.

****

SUNDAY MORNINGS

I think of them often
those who've gone away
especially on Sunday mornings
when we had coffee together
during phone calls from afar.

I think sometimes that when they left
they took part of me with them.
These days on Sunday mornings
when I relax with my coffee
I chat with them still.

Though sadly silent
these mental conversations
still evoke laughter in my heart.
I contemplate the wisdom of advice
I resented and never took
and now oddly miss.

Last Sunday morning I walked
in hills awash with flowers
when for a few moments butterflies
flitted playfully around my head;
delicate wings kissed my cheeks.

Again and again they returned,
wispy wings fluttering until finally
one lit upon my shoulder as if to ask,
"What shall we talk about today?"

"Oh, I miss you so," I whispered to the wind.

****

IN THIS PARK

It's been so many years since
we walked this path together.
Though you're no longer here
there are days I walk with you still
in this park where we often met.

At those times I feel you beside me
in quiet moments of solitary days;
I hear your laughter and your sighs
talks we shared through the years
moments I can't forget.

In my need you were always there.
How did I not recognize your pain
or the depth of your passions
unrealistic though they seemed?
Too late now to make amends.

Your presence was always so reliable;
then, without a hint, you were gone
Do you know I can feel you beside me?
The heart of you colors my reality;
so many beginnings and too-soon ends.

Now here in this park where we often met
I plant my tears in the earth.
Though not the place where you now rest
it is here I remember you best.

****

ONE TINY TEAR

If the trail of one tiny solitary tear
were to be traced up the cheek
onto which it has fallen
back into the eye and down
whatever path led it from the heart
where it was born and lived
until it was ejected into the world,
what story might be found
in that one tiny tear—
one of love and joy
or of torment and pain
which in any other circumstance
might fill an ocean
but is here condensed
by years of pressure
and now rolls from the eye
as the chest constricts
with all the effort required
to stifle a sob before
it is summarily eliminated
by the simple swipe
of the back of a hand
as if it never existed.

****

A SECRET

I sit alone at the table, a silver-framed
photograph of my beloved propped
in front of me.

The lights dim, music begins
and my attention, as everyone's,
turns to the rear of the room.

Doors snap open and there she stands
 her perfection so undeniable
as to elicit a collective gasp.

She glides languidly down the aisle;
her hips swing side to side with the
rhythmic regularity of a metronome.

Gleaming auburn tresses
cover her shoulders and back;
they sway with the grace
of a wheat field in a summer wind.

Her smile radiates a joy so complete
one is made to feel the warmth
of a loving embrace.

It is difficult to condemn.
Yet I, alone at this table long to hold
out my foot as she passes then grab her
by that gleaming hair before she hits the floor;

then with clenched fist, displace a few
pearly whites from that perfect smile
and thus radiate my own joy.

This is not the storied green-eyed monster,
but merely a quest for recompense
for the crushing blow, the pain in my heart.

I gaze again at the picture on the table;
tears spill down my cheeks as I recall the slow,
stealthy seduction that took him from me.

"Oh, man of my dreams, love of my life" I cry
in sworn silence, aware that only I know
this vixen before me used to be . . . him.

******

TEARS AND RAIN

It rained that Sunday.
It had been pending—
hanging in the air for weeks,
so heavy it dulled the senses.

Then everything went dark
and it came—the rain,
slow at first then harder.

I ran through that relentless
warm wet for an hour,
maybe more, both shivering
and sweltering in summer heat.

There was no shelter.
As suddenly as it began,
it stopped, leaving a silky grey mist.

In a store window my reflection
with the last drops of water
running down the glass
was a portrait of pathos.

You are gone but not the pain
and in that window
I couldn't tell my tears from the rain.

****

RAIN

Angry clouds gather, churn
and twist in a dull gray sky.

A woman sits in her room,
her back to the window,
hands gripping her chair,
oblivious to the pending storm.

It is midday but the sky is dark, still.
The breath of the world is caught
in its enormous throat. Suddenly
comes a distant growl of thunder,
a flash of lightning and the first drops
of rain begin to fall.

The woman is haunted by images
swirling in her head—barren desert,
a birth, a death, a blur of white flowers.
Searing, silent tears form in her eyes
and push their way over the edge.

The rain comes faster, pounding
the pavement, meadows, forests—
tears of the gods—falling
on devastated lands, to wash away
the sands of evil that cover its glory.

Claps of thunder shake buildings, trees;
lightning bolts sever the darkness.
The woman's tears flow, a turbulent sea;
her body quakes with sobs as her armor
cracks and disintegrates in the wake.

Rain and thunder, tears and pain
rage on in tempestuous battle.
Then, a new stillness—calm, serene.

A tiny glimmer of hope warms
the frail and faded flower of innocence
which perhaps in another time will
bloom once more.

****

GOODBYE

We've had 44 years together,
so much of our lives . . .
more than most really.
I thought it would be forever.
But time and circumstance
had other plans.

You've become depressed,
dismal and damaged
beyond my capacity to fix you.
You've devolved, deteriorated
become cold and hopeless.
No matter how hard I tried
none of my efforts rejuvenated
you; no act was ever enough.

Your dark and dreary mood
can no longer be overlooked.
The lack of sunshine in your heart
is unbearable for even one more day.

Truth is: I don't want you anymore.
Brutal though it seems, nothing about you
appeals to me any longer, a frightful fact
to face for I so loved you once . . .
but it's time to let you go.

I am moving on and I hope someone
will step in to slay your dragons
and learn to dwell in the depths of
your darkness.

And so . . . I close the door behind me
for the last time, breathe in the fresh
cool air as I walk down the path
to my car and drive away,
with never a backward glance.

Goodbye old house. Perhaps with
someone else, you will be reborn.

****

MY WISH FOR YOU

May the powers of the universe
instill in you always
pure joy in your existence

May good health always be yours
and may you be free to share
compassion and love along your path

May you learn and acquire knowledge
not only from formal education
but from every experience you have

May you be an active participant
in your time here on earth and understand
true success is not measured in dollars

And above all—may you know in your heart
that wherever you go and whatever you do
you are loved.

******

SKY & UNIVERSE

IF I COULD PAINT THE WAY SHE DOES

If I could paint the way she does
I would first dress in a flowing white robe
and wind flowers in my hair.
There would be soft music . . . with violins.

I would wash my canvas in a warm pale blue
the kind of blue that makes one smile
and dream of castles in the sky;
so would I begin.

I would dip a long slim artist's brush
into the whitest white paint and
holding it at arm's length from my canvas
I would twirl around and around
my arms waving with balletic grace
as I brush the canvas in sensuous swirls
of feathers and ferns and fragile fairies in flight.

I would dance and twirl as a summer wind
until the music reaches a crescendo
and in my final turn, I would dot a crescent moon
translucent on the remaining blue.

In this way would I replicate the sky
exactly as she presented it today
in that instant when it took my breath away—

 if I could paint the way she does!

****

THE CLOUD RIDER

On a wisp of cloud he rides
in white top hat & tails
Small in stature
straight and proud
an ebony baton in hand
With arms outstretched
he silently calls to the heavens
and at once the winds come
from every direction

Solid and strong
he stands ready to begin
He waves his black baton
in a flourish of infinity
and so conjoins and commingles
the winds, north with south,
east and west, strong with weak.

In that moment of shift
there comes a harmonious hum
as with hands and heart
the Cloud Rider conducts
the winds in a sweet
seductive symphony
and together they sing
joyfully to the Earth

When the people of Earth hear,
they abandon their greed,
hate and fear as the mighty winds
sing gloriously, united as one.

Satisfied, the Cloud Rider
lowers his black baton,
bows his head and is once more
a smiling, doddering old man
in a wheelchair.

****

IN A BLINK

How blue this day, the endless sky
from horizon to horizon
placid as a summer lake
yet empty as a broken heart

No puff of cloud dares the mind
to contemplate white sailed ships
cruising across the heavens
to the very limits of imagination

Envision the world upside down
the sky a barren tideless sea
all life burned away by relentless sun
which blazes from beneath

no visitor to its surface except
the chance ghostly passage of a single
cloud somehow familiar in form
which once called this place home

Consider two such amorphous puffs
of white as each takes its own shape
then fuses with the other to become
something entirely new, the old gone

no more nor less real than
what each was before
but changed forever
in the blink of an eye

And from above, what will rain
down that once lay buried
beneath the surface of this
now upended world

But today how blue the endless sky
tomorrow perhaps turbulent and gray
or full with bright clouds of inspiration
ever changing and evolving.

******

THE CLOUD FAIRIES

In the peaceful, quiet time just past daybreak, a woman enters her swimming pool to swim beneath the rising sun, a daily ritual. Afterward, she reclines in the water, her long hair fanned around her as she watches the blue above become more so.

Bright islands of clouds float like white ships in an endless sea of sky. She loses herself in the slow, graceful movement of the clouds as they twist and transform from one shape to another—animals, faces, illusions of places fantasized or remembered. She sees feathers, wings, and nonsensical things, and suddenly . . .

She's a child again, in the sandbox at a park, her mother on a bench behind her. On the lawn on the other side of the sandbox, an old man in a shabby brown coat and floppy hat sits alone on a green bench. He talks to himself, tittering like a mischievous child as he points to the sky.

When the child giggles, her mother leans close, whispers, "Stay away from that man. Don't laugh at him; he's not right." The child senses fear; she doesn't move but listens intently to hear the man's words as they float on the breeze toward the sandbox:

> *Oh, they're magical, fantastical,*
> *those cloud fairies—such tiny, fragile*
> *things, with their long white robes*
> *and transparent wings. They push*
> *the big clouds as they fly and paint*
> *their pictures in the sky.*

Then he laughs a laugh full of joy, his rheumy eyes bright with tears, bent finger still pointing up.

The child drops her pail and shovel and looks to the sky. Billowing clouds float gently past; small wispy ones move faster around them. Mesmerized, she watches as the big clouds magically transform into a glorious white castle, golden light streaming from windows in its fluffy walls.

And then, she sees them, the fairies, gaily flitting in and out and around it all. She gets to her feet and in her child's speechless excitement, jumps up and down and points skyward. She turns to tell the man, "Look . . . I see them" . . . but his bench is empty; the man is gone!

The mother looks up from her magazine. The child sits down, afraid to ask about the man.

From somewhere, the flat blare of a car horn rips her from her reverie. Still floating in the cool water, the woman watches the gleaming cumulus clouds form animated puffs of imagination; a smile creases her face as she recalls the gleeful laughter of a wrinkled old man in a floppy hat while her aging eyes scan the sky for a glimpse of the gossamer wings and flowing white robes of cloud fairies.

******

MARSHMALLOW TSUNAMI

The hills have lost their lavish
spring-summer luster
and taken on a more muted beauty
with an occasional surprise
of red and yellow wildflowers
which refuse to relinquish
their season of grandeur.

A wave of pure white cloud,
like a marshmallow tsunami,
oozes across what moments
ago was clear blue sky, and totally
obliterates every trace of blue.

If that were to roll over you,
would it be soft and warm
or harsh and frigid and might it
cause you to reach a grand epiphany
that opens your mind and enables you
to create hope and joy in the world
or would it simply be the quintessential
bad hair day which perpetuates insecurity
and fear, and precludes any sensible
progression of the reason for being.

Two long, beautiful white feather shapes
appear in a sudden patch of cerulean sky
and I know with complete certainty
they are stuck in the hat of some enormous
invisible being who is riding the wind
on a noble white horse called Cloud
and whistling "I've Got the World on a String. . ."

******

A BEDTIME STORY
(Or Just a Rough Night)

Thoughts tumble in a jumble
     as I lay restless in my bed.
Not relaxing is so darned taxing;
     I face a sleepless night with dread.
I try to quiet the erupting riot
     of ideas spinning round and round.
I count sheep in an attempt to sleep,
     and close my ears to sound.

In the dark I sense a spark
     of imagination in bloom.
An alien being from which I'm fleeing
     is right here in my room.
Just then it grabs me, forcefully drags me
     through a window, into the sky;
My brain says: "fight," but this thing might
     just drop me if I try.

I hang suspended, my life upended
     so unexpectedly,
when a thought occurs that's so absurd:
     Trust this force you cannot see!
Well, one would think that on the brink
     of looming liquidation,
one might say: "It's time to pray,"
     and start grooming for salvation.

But it's clear this isn't heaven
     and I'm sure it isn't hell;
the little tastes I've had of each
     have taught me pretty well.

Yet, I'm in the sky and don't know why;
     literally, hanging around
in the dead of night where stars are bright
     and the moon is full and round.

Clouds float by and I wonder if I
     can catch one and drift away
in this sea of sky, like Captain Bligh
     in the Pacific on that mutinous day.
As if on demand, an unseen hand
     deposits me on a cloud.
Will I sail this sea to my destiny?
     "HELP!" I cry out loud.

In my dire fright, I hold on tight
     as I hurtle through the sky
But I lose my grip and start to slip;
     I fear I'm going to die!
As I speed straight down toward the flat black ground,
     my life scrolls through my head.
There's a flash of light that's comet bright
     and I wake up in my bed.

****

The planets in our solar system revolve
around the sun whose gravity keeps them in
their orbits; similarly, the moon orbits Earth
as a result of the pull of Earth's gravity

GRAVITY

Consider, as you walk upon the ground
you're on the outside of a rock that's round
and hanging loose in the universe
The possibilities couldn't be worse

A force called "gravity" keeps us here
instead of floating free out there
It causes one thing and another
to move spontaneously toward each other

The sun is like the mother ship
She holds all the planets with a mighty grip
But if that mighty grip should slip . . .

    Oh, there's a gravity about gravity
    that can really bring you down

The mystical moon with its brilliant shine
is for lovers and poets—a muse divine
Earth's gravity holds that globe in place
If it stops—one muse lost in space

Romantics who would take a chance
in hopes they'll find their true romance
should know that alluring chemical attraction
is like the gravitational action

It's a similar magnetic event
and might make your life seem heaven-sent
But if that loving grip should slip . . .

Oh, there's a gravity about gravity
that can really bring you down

As years move on changes occur
Things don't stay where they once were
When gravity knocks upon your door
your parts start heading toward the floor

Such events will surely make you frown
but what goes up must come down
If gravity were not around
our feet would never touch the ground

So here we are, the human race
walking on our great Earth's face
But if that powerful grip should slip . . .

Oh, there's a gravity about gravity
that can really bring you down

****

Facts: The planet Venus is hot, full of fire
and volcanoes; it rotates clockwise while all
the other planets rotate counterclockwise.

VENUS RISING

I saw her last night through the haze,
when she was the only visible light;
always the brightest of the bright
except for Mother Moon.

Mist obscured all but her sparkling
Splendor as she floated
just above the tiniest silver
sliver of Mother Moon.

I decided we should chat, Ms. Venus and I.

"Tell me," said I, "are you here to impart
to we earthlings all the goodies guided
by that glorious Roman goddess for whom
you are named—you know, love, beauty,
prosperity, fertility, and of course, wild sex?

"I am not the keeper of Earth or its people
but honestly, we are in pretty desperate need
of some of that stuff over which your
eponymous goddess reigned.

"You need not worry about prostitution
which was also within her purview;
we have enough problems without that."

Now I didn't plan to be pushy because
I didn't know much about Venus
except from what I'd read but, you know,
a person doesn't often get an opportunity
like this.

It's not like she makes such a bold appearance
on a regular basis. So, I continued:

"I get that you have your own challenges,
being the only female planet, but since
you are way hotter than those "guys"
and can be pretty toxic—AND you move
in opposing circles,

"I just wonder if you might have the time
and inclination to help us out down here.
We sure could use a boatload of love if you
can manage it. If you give us that, we can
probably handle the other stuff ourselves."

Now I'm fairly certain I saw her wink or blink
though maybe it was me since I was pretty tired
but I know she brightened for a few seconds—
just before she slipped behind the curtain
of mist and disappeared.

I hope I didn't overstep.

******

CONSTANT COMPANION

In the dark, I see you
my constant companion
most trusted confidante
though on this night
only your welcoming smile
is visible on that face
I've known through all the years
of secret conversations.

In the early bright of today
before clouds gathered
I saw you, ghost-like,
transparent as tissue paper
yet I felt your presence
saw the familiar grin—
Cheshire-like but gentler
more loving and guileless.

Now in night's growing chill
mist unlights the stars
as trees cast shadows on clouds
and streetlights illuminate
only their own casings.

Yet as I see the perfect crescent
of your smile, wreathed
by a rainbow aura, I am reminded
that you are now, have been
and always will be
right there no matter what.

******

THE FACE

The sun was shining
when I first saw
the blurred round face
with smudged eyes
and a tilted half-smile.

It hovered just above the treetops,
peered through the branches
at people on the boulevard, at me.
It watched, quiet, reflective, God-like.

Later, I hurried along through
semi-dark streets when a sensation
of something behind me caused me to turn
and there it was again, the face,
aglow in the near dark, watching.

Curiously unafraid, I dallied.
It stopped, silently waited.
When I began again on my way,
it followed me all the way home.

Once inside, I sat in the dark
while outside my window,
the face inched slowly upward.
It continued to watch me
with its dark Svengali eyes
as a million stars glittered around it.

Suddenly I wanted desperately
to be with that face, to float free
in the vastness of the universe,
far from the chaos of this world.

At that moment, shafts of silver
sprang from the face, moved toward me
and passed through my window
as I stood motionless, mesmerized.

Icy cold, yet searing hot shiny beams
surrounded, penetrated, filled
and transformed me into an explosion
of brilliant shimmering light.

I glided through the glass
into the sparkling heavens
and flew on wings of air and light
filled with a carefree bliss
and became a part of everything that is.

Sweet nearly inaudible music
filtered through the dark to my brain
and I heard a voice, THE voice,
"Fly me to the . . ." and wow!
I knew he would be here.

Gradually, the music got louder,
everything got brighter as my eyes
opened to streaks of morning light.

A new day had begun.

****

THE MOON FELL

What remained of the waning moon
hung heavy, a swollen silver basket
so overfilled and bottom-heavy
it looked ready to tear away
from the winter night sky.

This magnificent gleaming bowl
was in the direct line of my sight
as I drove the dark highway to home.

Dark clouds cast ominous silent shadows
that crept across the silver while the rows
of reflectors on the unlit highway dimmed
demanding more concentration
and each time I looked up it was lower,
that bowl—bigger—heavier.

And
        then
                it
                      fell.

It fell into the mountains and I could see it
through the trees pulsing slow,
slower and slower like ET's heart
in that gut-wrenching scene in the movie
and the glow that rose above the treetops
faded—faded until it was gone and I felt
a tightening in my chest and my eyes
burned and I shouted at the fallen moon,

"No, please

      STAY
             Stay
                    stay!"

But it was gone and the sky
was a starless, dull black blanket,
the only light headlamps of passing cars,
the only sound wheels spinning
on dry rough asphalt.

It was a sound of emptiness enhanced
by unfathomable feelings of loss, fear, isolation.

I pressed hard on the accelerator
with an urgent need for

home
       bed
              sleep
                     peace.

And there I wept, wept for the fallen moon,
for loss, for the departed. I wept and then I slept.

And quietly, gently, night drifted
into bright morning, and I walked
in sunshine. Leaves of burnished gold
rained down upon me in a warm breeze
and in the sky—in a clear blue sky,
barely visible, floated the ghost
of the fallen moon, not gone, a celestial
symbol of presence more than memory,
of those we love.

****

SOUL OF NIGHT

O dark and empty sky
where is your soul
that lights the night,
missing now for days.

Has it forever turned
its back on this world
and left us in such
profound darkness
that even the stars
are extinguished.

In this black void
memory of the profound
artistry of your light
permeates the senses
a lesson that when souls depart
the essence of their beauty
is more defined
to those who remain.

******

WHAT THE MOON SAID

Just after the moon sent
the last superstorm and tsunami
to earth and was gearing up
to hurl meteor-sized ice balls
to cause freezing snowy squalls
in the warmest regions of our planet
all in an effort to get our attention
I heard it say:

"You know, they've been here
from the start. They were the first.
Some rose from the center
of the earth, some from the sea—
alive, though their life force
was nearly invisible, but alive
nonetheless.

"But you humans, so smug in your
ignorance, completely convinced
that all intelligent life looks like you,
so clueless that all life has its own
complex method of communication.
You just don't see.

"The mountains hold the truth of
everything that ever occurred—
the real truth of creation, and what
will remain after humans are gone.
If the vegetation stops breathing,
you will too; it all communicates
with each other, and you humans,
you just poison it all, completely
unaware you're poisoning yourselves.

"This beautiful Earth is more than
four and a half billion years old
and it's damned tired of your disrespect.
In fact, the entire universe is pretty
pissed off that all the warnings have
been ignored—hence, the superstorms,
tsunamis, earthquakes.

"Get a grip, humans, before the sun
and I let go and your precious planet
goes flying into oblivion."

That's what the moon said but no one
was listening . . . except me. I tried to tell
some of you but hell,
        no one listens to me either.

****

THE WAY THE MOON RISES

Have you ever thought about
the way the moon rises—

How at first it is barely visible
then seems to peek over the horizon
to see what awaits its arrival
as it swells in blazing light
and dares you not to look at it
in awe-stricken wonder.

Have you ever noticed the belly
of an expectant mother

How it is first barely visible
then grows slowly while the mother waits
then proceeds to blossom full
and round for all to see
and dares you not to look at it
in awe-stricken wonder.

Have you ever really thought about
the way the moon rises?
I have.
I just watch in awe-stricken wonder.

****

WHEN A STAR IS BORN

It happens all the time
A star appears from nowhere
like a dream come to life
or perhaps a nightmare

The star glows and grows until
it shines with incomparable light
so intense it catches fire
and burns from the inside out

Still burning, it spins out of control
into the infinite universe
where after a time it cools
and completely turns to ash
Or if it is strong at its core
it creates a new light
and is reborn to shine again

Such is the way of the world—
in the heavens and on earth
When a star is born.

****

SPEAKING OF THE STARS

Someone once said if a person
were to stand beneath a certain
stellar constellation, as Orion's belt,
the stars within it will blink
in syncopation with a song
and send a musical signal
straight to that person's cerebrum.

It seemed to me that someone should
do some research to see if that is so
since it sounds silly to suggest
a strip of stars could simply shine
and somehow send such a signal
upon receipt of which said person
would unconsciously start to dance.

Too stubborn and cynical to accept
such a suggestion, super sleuth that I am,
one night I surreptitiously slipped outside
and stood silently in the dark beneath
that very constellation.

Almost instantly my certainty started to slip
as I began subtly to swirl and sway
to a song that steadily circled
around and around in my head.

Since then, I have come to strongly support
the hypothesis that the stars might
disseminate secret yearnings deep inside us.

Perhaps that is what spurred President
Theodore Roosevelt to say,

> "Keep your eyes on the stars
> and your feet on the ground."

So, what do you say?

******

THE GREAT OUTDOORS

MOTHER NATURE

Inhale the glory of nature
from dawn to dawn
mountain to sea
forest to desert.

Absorb her essence
with hungry eyes
through each pore of your skin
every fiber of your being.

Listen . . . her music is for you
her precious lover.
Smell her perfume—
the spicy sweetness of love's bouquet.

Concede that in her presence
there is no doubt
that you and God are one.

****

NATURE THERAPY

Everyone has a day sometimes
when nothing is going right
and people all around you
are spoiling for a fight.

You need someone to talk to,
sympathetic company.
Here's the best advice I've heard:
Go out and hug a tree.

Take yourself away from
the dissension and despair.
Go for a run or a brisk walk
out in the fresh air.

If you need something to lean on
when life's not as it should be
go to a park and look around
for the biggest tallest tree.

Tell it all your troubles
until your mind is completely bare.
Ignore the smirking passers-by
who watch you standing there.

The tree has long stood its ground
unfettered through the years.
It won't flinch or judge you
on the reason for your tears.

It has survived more harsh storms
than most people ever do
has been a haven for so much life
and now perhaps for you.

Just put your ear close to its heart
and listen carefully.
Be still—receive its wisdom.
It's telling you: *Just Be*!

****

MORNING IN THE WOODS

It must have been divine direction
that brought me to this place
among giant trees that have been here
long before my entry onto this plane

The sense of peace here fuels
the imagination of this city girl
whose ignorance of the existence
of these woods boggles the mind

The whoosh of water bubbling
over rocks in a nearby brook
is a love song to my heart
and entertains me as I walk
on clouds of spongy earth
to the foot of a towering oak
whose low-slung branches
invite a climb into its heights

The slow tentative ascent
to the higher branches
intoxicating perfume of the woods
water-song of the brook
and gentle rustle of leaves
are contradictions of everything
I've thought of as "civilized"

I sit on a slightly swaying branch
high in the canopy of this tree
as the sun burns higher and brighter
and sends rays of light through
the greenery to cast a spotlight on me

I am the conductor of nature's ballet
Leaves and grass dance in the breeze
The brook sings to forest sprites
and wood nymphs I imagine frolicking
on the ground among the trees

In such sacred perfection I am filled
with joy and promise and the knowledge
that almost anything is possible—

    if I don't encounter a bear.

****

A WALK IN THE WOODS

I wander through lush woods, entranced
by the perfect symmetry of each tree
when at the edge of my path
I watch two young trees sway gracefully,
branches entwined in a leafy embrace—
young lovers slow dancing in the breeze.

In the quiet beauty of this communion
the whispered sound of leaves all around,
in the air, on the ground, urges me on
into the greener depths of this forest
past a triad of white-barked birch,
trunks braided together.

I follow a soft spongy path of fallen leaves
and twigs to a dark grove, a veritable orgy
of spiraling contorted trunks and tangled
limbs, so connected that where one begins
or another ends, is indeterminate.

I am smitten by the peaceful perfection,
the gentle rustle of leaves, the only sound,
the total connectivity of every living thing
oblivious of my intrusion as life goes on
giving, nurturing, sustaining . . . life.

******

DROUGHT

Another blazing day in this valley;
no rain to speak of for nearly a year.
It must have been wishful thinking
on the part of the park rangers when
they lined the canyon trail with sandbags.
Some might see that as a guarantee
it won't rain, just as washing one's car
seems a guarantee it will.

It's Spring and these hills should be green
and lush, ablaze with colorful wildflowers.
Instead, they are barren, bleached almost
white by relentless sun.

And the trees, the once glorious trees . . .
some lay broken and shriveled on the ground.
Others stand dry and gray. Leafless. Lifeless.
Sagging branches are slightly upturned
as though praying for liquid life from the sky.

And woodland creatures—few are present;
not even one of the usually plentiful lizards.
No snakes. No rabbits. No birds. A scruffy
solitary squirrel scampers up a lifeless tree
then down—up again and down.

I read once that squirrels can remember
for almost three years where they've
stashed their food but this one seems
confused—this tree is unrecognizable.

It seems that Mother Nature
has abandoned her children.

Higher in the hills, the desolation
is even worse. Fallen trees lay
dismembered and rotting.
My eyes fill with tears and overflow.

As if my tears will make a difference.

****

A TREE'S PRAYER

Amidst bare, brittle, battered bones
of those that came before,
a rainbow of green graces the hills.
Profusions of yellow, purple, and red
flowers dance in the breeze.

And I, once strong and mighty,
still stand tall as I gasp for breath,
thirst unquenchable despite recent rains,
desperate to heal my burnt, broken boughs
for the sake of my offspring that cling
precariously to my withering heart.

Mother, why did you abandon us
and now return to view the dead
and dying among us.
Oh, creator and destroyer of life
we have seen you work your magic—
birth a tiny flower from the depths
of lands you decimated by fire and ash.

Forgive my anger for I am grown
yet still your child who like all children
both love and loathe my creator.
For all that remain here
I implore you, have mercy.

Give us nourishment enough that
a new generation may survive.
We have lived long lives but now
grow weaker with each day.

I pray thee be now creator not destroyer.
Protect us, that our children may flourish.

****

DEAR OLD FRIEND

I went to visit a dear old friend.
Injury had kept me away
and in the interim extreme
dry weather had damaged
the surrounding landscape.

As I trudged up the steep hill
to where she lived, I felt
I was returning home
and at first sight of her, I ran,
excited to throw myself
into the curve of her arms
before I realized how gray,
broken and brittle she was.

Long my companion and solace
in times of need, this old oak tree,
my dear friend had suffered
the lethal effects of lingering drought
and now, in what would have been
her season of greatest beauty
she stood dry and naked
as in the depths of winter.

Her branches which had enfolded
me like a mother's arms, now
adorned only by a few dry leaves
which fluttered to the ground
at the slightest hint of breeze,
were unable to hold me.

Thinking back, she had been weak
at my last visit; her few offspring
had lain dormant around her.
I brought water, as much as I could carry

in an effort to save them and cursed
the evil that caused this devastation.

During my absence, the rains came,
heavy and continuous—but too late.
It was obvious that soon my friend
like others around her would fall
and ultimately return to the earth.

I hope and feel in my heart that one day
she or her progeny will live again
because life always seems to find its way.

****

TODAY IT RAINED

The air's been thick.
Heavy. Dulls the senses.
And gray. The air.
The sky. The world.

Sometimes a sadness
slips in on days like this
and slows a body down
like a good friend who
shows up to calm you
when life gets stormy.
Sometimes that sadness
is good company.

But not today.

Today a fierce energy
slipped in, unexpected.
A freight train rumbled
across the heavens, sent
silver streaks of electricity
to sever the gray and finally,
after this long drought—

Today it rained!

******

JUST ADD WATER

Grimy gray clouds and fog cast a
ghostly gloom over the city. Dry
barren hillsides and brittle
brown lawns parched by
relentless summer sun
create a study in sepia.

Endless dreary, dismal days,
of murky mist pervade the air
until cleansing rain begins to fall;
it hammers roofs and sidewalks,
saturates fields and hills for three days,
then slows to gentle shower and stops.

Morning bursts forth in glittering sunshine
which bounces off still-wet green leaves
on trees yesterday lifeless and limp—dying.
The once-brown hillsides and lawns boast
carpets of new grass fine as babies' hair.

Mother Nature has done it again
Her recipe for rebirth?
Just add water.

****

FIRE

What veil of evil sweeps across
the land to dull the sun's shine
and ejects living pieces of itself
to spark and flare into frantic tongues
that lick hungrily at the tops of trees;
then tempted by the taste devours
everything in its path and leaves
in its wake charred chunks of debris
as a mythical Christmas spirit
leaves lumps of coal to dash the hopes
of naughty children.

Malignant flame-breathing monster
that you are, as you suck the very air
from our already woe-filled world,
know you are victor for only a moment
for our warriors have before and will again
crush you and will rise ever stronger,
as a Phoenix, from the ashes of your destruction.

******

AFTER

There are no flowers on this hillside
only hard-packed earth
bruised and battered
neither giving nor softening
in the season's storms

No boulders to cling to or lean upon
only young saplings that struggle
for their own survival
and too easily bend
to the will of the wind

Winged emissaries of grace and beauty
collect seeds from far-off gardens
then soar into the clouds
and drop their bounty into hidden
pockets of that hardened heart
which will one soon tomorrow
burst with bountiful blossoms
of flowers and trees to nourish
the earth and banish forever
from memory this barren hillside

****

THE FLOWERS OF YOUTH

Once upon a time
when we were young
we listened to the wisdom
of flowers of the field
and believed there was magic
in what they told us.

Buttercups suggested if we
saw a bright yellow reflection
when we held them to our chins
we liked butter and there
was beauty within us.

Dandelions when they went
to seed were like exotic genies
who would grant wishes if we
blew their delicate white fronds
into the wind.

Daisies most loved even secretly
by boys were the surefire way
to know if the person we loved
loved us in return as we pulled
their petals one by one.

Honeysuckle if we sucked its stem
or chewed its flowers always
delivered its sweet nectar but
we were warned not to eat the berries
lest we get a tummy ache.

Most coveted was the four-leafed clover
a rare treasure to keep forever for
the luck it promised was as valuable
as the pot of gold at a rainbow's end.

Now, so many years later
I still smile at the pretty buttercups
savor the sweet taste of honeysuckle
and pick daisies, though loves
like the petals have come and gone.

I still make dandelion wishes
just for fun with the same exuberance
as in my youth and search the grass
these days with my grandchildren
for that ever-elusive four-leafed clover.

****

*Every living thing has its time, its season,
when it is at its best. To find its season
it must experience them all. This is true
for plants, human beings, and animals
of every kind. It is this fact that connects
all life ....Ecclesiastes 3:1*

HAD I NOT NOTICED

Had I not noticed the massive tree
in spring with buds of new life
straining against yesterday's
protective shell to soon explode
into summer splendor
its verdant leaves and fragrant blooms
reaching toward the sun

and had I not noticed when its
colors changed and its leaves
tore away one by one in autumn
to lay dry and brittle on the ground
even while its powerful frame
clad only in dull gray bark
was still ready to brave
the angry temperaments of winter

had I not noticed all that I wonder
would I still have recognized
the strength of its heart
which weathers the erosive elements
of time to perpetuate its beauty?

****

SUMMER

Early memories of shadowy grunge
of the Bronx streets of my childhood
elicit pictures of colorless seasons,
bare cement sidewalks,
faded tan tenement buildings,
corner lots filled with Quonset huts
inhabited by poor families,
mostly of war veterans unable to work
who in my child's mind, all seemed
to have too many children.

Winters didn't see many people
on the streets. The few trees
in the area were bare.
Snow and chill and muddy slush
were everywhere.

Spring was a bit brighter
due to the plethora of yellow
dandelions and occasional
buttercups, though the few trees
sprouted little worthy of mention;
and

Autumn was nothing like colorful
pictures described in songs;
leaves that fell were already brown.

It was only in the summer,
when the heat and humidity
were nearly unbearable,
the blazing sun reflected
off bumpers of passing cars,

and some blessed soul, most often
a policeman, took pity on us kids
and wrenched open a fire hydrant
letting cool, clean water flood out,
that the streets came fully alive
with the laughter of children together—
brown and black and white bodies
glistening wet and slippery, all joining
in the dance of Summer.

****

SAILING

What is this feeling so strange to me,
this sweet/salt taste of being free.

I'm all alone but so at ease,
a daughter of the sea and breeze.

This is life as life should be.
The sky, the sea, the breeze and me.

****

AUTUMN

Mountains are shrouded in morning mist.
Birds congregate on high wires
as before a storm though no storm is near—
perhaps to decide if their winter flight south
will be by a quick or scenic route.

Butterflies surreptitiously listen in.
They might leave as well but more likely,
will choose to rest in crevices of logs
or beneath loose bark in trees
until warm days return.

On the ground, squirrels gather nuts
and acorns, chipmunks are hard at work
to find seeds and berries, to store in nests
for coming cold days, while in the woods,
young bucks end summer bachelor soirees,
their soft antlers of youth having hardened;
they are ready to test their virility against
Summer friends now turned rivals
for attention of the most attractive does.

In other parts of the forests and fields,
bears, skunks, chipmunks, and even snakes,
greedily gorge themselves in preparation
for their substantial "don't bother me until
Spring" hibernation.

Days are still warm but nights have cooled
and though grass is still mostly green,
Autumn is confirmed by shorter days
and coloring of leaves not yet fallen.
Hillsides are ablaze with rainbow vistas

as summer growth of flowers, trees, and vines
begin to fade until, like the bears,
they will soon find their winter rest.

And we humans are mesmerized
by Mother Nature's magic even as
we watch enticing pumpkin patches
decorated with scarecrows, black cats,
witches and amusement rides pop up
on busy street corners where local farmers
sell their wares for excited children
to create scary or funny jack-o-lanterns
for Halloween—until we begin to complain
about the chill when Winter once again is here.

But for now, we breathe the cool fresh air,
enjoy the luscious landscape, walk beneath
trees and catch falling leaves or if we're lucky,
luxuriate in a lavender shower as the last
of the Jacaranda blossoms, float to earth.

Or, we can head to the woods and try
to watch the bucks go at it.

****

WOODLAND MAGIC

During a walk in the woods
I by chance unearth a piece of bone
buried beneath dry leaves.
It is smooth and silky as time
and the elements tend to alter things.

I enclose it in my palm
and sit upon a fallen log
to examine it more closely
when I sense movement
in the brush behind me.

I turn to see the face of a tiny fawn,
head tilted ears twitching
as if to hear my thoughts.
Its clear eyes meet mine,
curious as a human child.

As its tender young nose
pushes closer through the brush
a huge stag with regal antlers
appears and nudges it away.

With the now warm piece of bone
in my fist I envision myself face to face
with a giant elk who surveys me
much as the young fawn did.

I stand on tiptoe and run trembling fingers
along the smooth surface of his antlers
when my hand comes to rest on the pedicle,
the bump at their base, the root
from which they grow.

I feel a vibration of life strong and powerful.
The elk's eyes inform he will not harm me
nor does he fear me but he backs away
then turns and sprints into eternity.

Late afternoon light plays tricks
on my eyes. Dappled sunlight creates
shadows like animals moving
from tree to tree.

I drop the piece of bone back
onto the forest floor and wind my way
through the trees to return
to my world of mundane reality.

****

WINTER WOODS

I ran one day through winter woods.
	Dry leaves covered the ground,
crackling beneath my running shoes.
	I heard no other sound.

Shards of sunlight pierced the trees
	like golden arrows from Cupid's bow;
and on a verdant hill ahead
	the trees appeared to glow.

On that far hill awash with light
	a silhouette took shape
of a man in perfect archer's stance.
	I watched, my mouth agape.

I ran to the hill, climbed to the top
	so curious was I;
and there he stood, a half-clad man—
	a banquet to my eye.
A light around his presence glowed
	though mortal he appeared to be;
his movements caused the wind to sing
	and I trembled when he looked at me.

Now I'd know Cupid anywhere
	but no winged cherub did I see;
and this perfect sculpted god-like man
	most certainly wasn't he.

So stunned was I, no words came forth;
	my mouth felt filled with sand.
Struck dumb I lowered my eyes to find
	a sunbeam in my hand.

He plucked the sunbeam from my hand
        and with no malice I could see,
he threaded it in his twisted bow, then
        aimed it straight at me.

With eyes tight closed I stood tall and
        proud like St. Joan at the stake
and told myself *If this is a dream,
        now's the time to wake.*

And wake I did to chilling wind,
        leaves swirling all around;
no man, no cupid, no golden glow
        only me upon the ground.

Darkness had begun to fall;
        where the time went, I don't know.
I looked around and against a tree
        I saw . . . the twisted bow.

Cautiously I picked it up
        and held it close to me.
The chill wind stopped, the air grew still
        and a warmth washed over me.

It's been some time since that day
        but I notice more and more
real beauty in the simplest things
        I hadn't seen before.

I believe in this frenetic world
        there's still more love than hate
and I hope it's true that good things come
        to those of us who wait.

This tale won't be believed by some
    though every word is so
for in my dreams there is no end
    to the places I can go.

Still, I run each day in the winter woods
    looking for that man
and chasing sunbeams with a child's hope
    to hold one in my hand.

****

THE ARRIVAL

For too many days the chill
had been too difficult to bear
Gray clouds filled the sky
Sidewalks were snow-covered
Much life succumbed to icy gloom

A tiny crocus somehow pushes
its little yellow head through the snow
and creates an unexpected light
a smile in the midst of sadness
a prelude to the coming Spring

Lion and lamb reconcile
Chrysalis morphs into butterfly
despair into rhapsody of joy and hope
and in an instant darkness becomes light

The dreary world is a symphony
of red, white, gold, and green
as in what seems overnight
trees and flowers birth new life
in a blaze of color and fragrance

Bears, bats, chipmunks, squirrels
come out of winter hideaways
to find mates and proceed
as Mother Nature has directed
Love is everywhere

Spring has arrived!

****

I AM

Once I was a cloud
afloat in the space
between there and here
I faded into nothingness

Once I was the earth
a blue spec in the universe
orbiting an uncaring sun
It lost its grip and let go

And once I was a snail
on the ocean's shore
enticed into a wave to ride the tides
into a thousand tomorrows

Today I am drawn from
forest's edge into its depths
by whisper of breeze through boughs
a language of rippling grace

The clean green scent of the air
solitude of sunlight through treetops
and splendiferous silence
speak karmically to my heart

I am free simply to be
We breathe life into one another
the trees and me and in these moments
as never before

    I am
        I Am
            I AM

****

HIKING TO FOREVER

My footsteps set a rhythm;
the rhythm changes the way I move.
Stride becomes dance: and 1 and 2,
and 3 and 4, and 1 and 2 and 3 and 4.

For a further distraction from the sun's
relentless heat on my hatless head
I include my heartbeat: duh-dum and 2
and 3 and 4, duh-dum and 2 and 3 and 4.

I extend my arms and in my mind,
I pirouette once and twice and
three and four, then run into a flying
split-leap with unbridled joy up
this steep, precarious ridge trail.

I high-five the lush leafy branches
that brush me as I pass until finally
I reach the summit after three miles
of hot, sweaty uphill.

I chug-a-lug half a bottle of Crystal
Geyser, pour the rest on my head
while I absorb the 360-degree view.

Forever is almost visible in every
direction from here—beyond
the billowing cushions of clouds above,
beyond the dark depths of the canyon
whose walls fall away from the sides
of this narrow ridge, and beyond
the still snow-capped peaks far off
in the distance.

Forever is magnificent; I just know it.
I turn around slowly, once and once more,
here, on this ridge which feels like
the top of the world and I'm dancing again.

I'm dancing on the edge of forever
and . . .
        I Feel So Freaking Free!

****

MAN WATCHING

We hike the curves and steep hills
of the canyon, my good friend and I,
whenever we can find time.
We do it because exercise is good,
it's healthy, fun, and we get to hang out
and indulge in a favorite pastime.

This particular canyon is frequented
at all hours of the day by hip young
Hollywoodians, both men and women,
all sizes, shapes, and colors,
strenuously strutting their stuff
in varying stages of . . . undress.

The women, though not our
frequent focus, wear strategically
torn workout clothes, while the men—
ahh, the men—are mostly shirtless,
and sport serious six or eight-packs
on smooth, strong, sexy, sweaty bodies.

We are voyeurs in plain sight;
we delight in the display of hard
rounded rear ends that might fit
in even the most feminine hand
with the solidity of a shot-put,
wide muscular shoulders and backs
forming a perfect "V" shape from
shoulder to hip.

And of course, there are those
ready for the silver screen faces
with their bright smiles and perfect teeth,
heads of glossy stylish hair—long, short, shaved.

My friend hungers in an almost feral
frenzy for one of these tasty treats.
He is much more likely to meet the man
of his dreams here than I.

****

THE MAGIC OASIS

Five friends trek up a steep rocky trail
ten thousand feet up in the Sierra Mountains
accompanied by a warm, welcome breeze.

In pain but determined, I push on, two small
fractured bones in my foot be damned, but
after two torturous miles, my fortitude fizzles.
I decide to wait while my friends continue further.

I wander across a creek, through a stand
of pine trees, to the lush green shore
of a heart-shaped lake surrounded by towering
granite peaks sculpted into sensuous curves
and dips by Mother Nature's own hand after
she birthed them from sea and land.

Barefoot, I sit at the shoreline, my feet dangling
in the icy cold of this magnificent blue-green
lake, entertained by throngs of tiny sun fairies
who dance gaily upon the ripples in the water.
I watch them jump and twirl as on tiptoe they
pirouette en masse toward me, surround my
sore and swollen feet, and with their sparkling
magic, set my pain adrift.

Renewed and energized, shoes laced back on,
I walk around the banks, back to the creek
marveling at every shrub and rock and tree,
absorbing the power of this mountain oasis.

I hoist myself onto a boulder and turn my face
to the sun as the breeze first whispers then
serenades me into a trance.

I am at the very beginning, the first of my kind,
basking in the breathtaking beauty of the garden.

In this moment there is perfect peace in the world,
in me, and I am thrilled there is no deceitful snake
to tempt me into the tempest of that other time.

****

SOLE PATTERNS

Some days a random thought rolls around in your head and you don't have a clue as to where it came from. On other days you see something and the proverbial light bulb illuminates in an invisible bubble just above you, a sort of "Eureka moment" like in a cartoon.

That happened to me one day as I walked around the track at the local park, a mile trek—a decent walk if the half-mile each way from home and back is considered.

On the short straight path that leads to the track, I noticed a plethora of unique imprints in the dirt, made by shoes of the multitudes of men, women, and children who regularly walk or run on this track.

That was the moment when that light bulb lit. Those were "sole" patterns or "soul" patterns. There were so many different ones, pointed in various directions, as if each pair was trying to find its best path.

Just for the heck of it, I checked the imprints made by my shoes—a fairly unique, waffle-like design, very distinct with numerous very defined separate compartments.

I decided to try to locate one pair of footprints I could follow completely around the track. The effort became sort of a mini-meditation.

It was almost a half hour before I found a consistently uniform set of footprints that didn't abruptly disappear into oblivion. They were fairly small, probably made by a young boy who had been running, based on the distance between the prints and their depth, as if it took some impact to make them.

I followed them about halfway around the track where they stopped, pivoted, and went back the way they came still uniformly strong. I followed them part of the way back, then turned again and did my own loop around the track.

When I neared where I began my walk, I attempted to find my own very distinct imprints in the dirt. They were gone, not hidden among the many others, just gone, as though I'd never been there.

Closer to where I had first entered the track, I found a few still barely visible; that light bulb flashed on again . . . the universe had just told me I should have another go around because I didn't leave a lasting impression the first time.

****

SKI SEASON

A NON-SKIER'S VIEW OF SKI SEASON

Phantom skiers on summer slopes
feed the dreams and raise the hopes

of those who await the winter show
of those same slopes dressed in pure white snow

They'll don their ski clothes and ride the lifts
and then schuss down those icy drifts

But I will follow a different trend
and stay warm in bed with a lusty friend.

******

FANTASY SKIING
(Or Taking It To The Slopes)

I asked friends how it feels to ski
        to gather information.
They used words like "indescribable"
        and "great exhilaration."

I took their words and thoughts
        deep into my imagination
to parallel their experience with
        what could cause me such elation.

So if you will indulge me
        I think you'll have some fun
and I will take you all with me
        on my fantasy virgin run . . ..

I push off from the mountaintop
        and gently down I glide,
very tentative at first,
        I move from side to side.

My breath comes out in little clouds;
        I feel the winter chill,
but as graceful as I dancer
        I am skiing down this hill.

I think: *this is not so tough*
        I think I've got the knack;
I'm not sure where I'm going
        but I know I can't turn back.

I'm moving somewhat faster now;
        I'm not ready for this yet.
That little chill has gone away
        and I've begun to sweat.

I see some moguls up ahead,
        my heart begins to pound.
I angulate my hips and thighs
        with every up and down.

My breath comes fast; my feet dig in
        and oh, my knees are weak.
I feel I'm losing all control
        and I let out a shriek.

I'm streaking down the mountain
        through a blur of haze and mist
and life on the periphery
        is ceasing to exist

Suddenly I'm airborne—
        I can hardly breathe at all.
For a moment I'm suspended
        and then I start to fall.

The fall gives way to floating
        the air smells musky sweet.
My breathing slows to normal;
        I land gently on my feet

The air has now grown cooler
        and I shiver with the chill
and ponder what just happened
        as I look back at the hill.

There's something so familiar
        that I just can't place but then
there is one thing I know for sure—
        I want to go again!

******

FANTASY SKIING 2
(Maximum Exposure)

It's been some time since my virgin run
        and just of late I find
I have a need to return to the slopes
        if only in my mind

I close my eyes and images
        of snowy mountains soar
taking me back to the wonder
        of that place I knew before

Except . . . the mountains look much
        taller now and damn, I feel so small
I'm plagued by insecurity
        Can I do this at all

So, I remember how much fun I had
        and how I felt inside
in an attempt to strengthen my resolve
        Now I'm ready for my ride

I meditate, I concentrate—
        I put my fear on hold
No snowplow or bunny slopes for me
        I'm going for the gold

Except . . . the mountain towers above me
        like Damocles' sharp sword
but the chairlift beckons beguilingly
        Will I dare to climb aboard

I pull on my bravado pants
        jet black and spandex-tight
then my heavy bold front shirt—
        make sure it's buttoned right

My bright red scarf of courage
     around my neck to keep me warm
Its ends fly like wings behind me
     and keep me safe from harm

My boots and skis locked on my feet
     my poles are digging in
I reach the lift and take a seat
     then sit back with a grin

It seems to take forever until
     we finally reach the summit
And now the only thing I see
     is a cliff from which I'll plummet

I watch the other skiers
     one by one take off with grace
And now it is my turn to shine—
     I show a brave and happy face

I fly off the first mogul and land
     in a tight crouch on the ground
I think *finally, I'm home free*
     when I hear a dreadful sound

My bravados split both front and back
     and are hanging at my knees
My bold front pops its buttons
     and is flapping in the breeze

The cold wind whips around me
     and my courage comes unwound
and lands somewhere behind me
     a red splotch on the ground

My confidence has blown away
        and of my clothes I am bereft
But determination will get me home
        with what strength I have left

The finish looms before me
        oh gosh I'm going to make it
And a crowd is cheering—
        not for my skill, but because . . .

I'M OUT HERE SKIING NAKED!

****

IF I WERE SNOW

On a crisp cold mountain night
when the sky above is clear and bright
and the entire Milky Way on high
is a silver smudge against black sky

you'd look up and watch in thrall
as I pretend, I'm the stars and start to fall
first like stardust all around
then sparkling as I reach the ground

I'd gently melt into your skin
and make you tingle from within
My touch would set your heart on fire
until you're burning with desire

You'd pray for my presence all around
to cover every inch of ground
If I felt your lust for me was true
Well, hell, of course I'd fall for you

******

THE LEGEND OF OLD BEN
(In Memory of John Perkins)

PROLOGUE:
After a happy day of skiing
        to a bar we all were fleeing
with a thirst for beer and cheerful
        chat about the day gone by.
With hopes for fun activity
        our most natural proclivity
we sat around and chatted
        'til the very last keg was dry.

So, when we looked out in the snow
        and saw a figure all aglow
moving down the tallest mountain
        at a startling rate of speed,
it didn't give us pause
        we just assumed the cause
was all the brew which of course we knew
        we had consumed in our greed.

Soon Big John P. pulled up a chair
        He ran his fingers through his hair
and made a decision about our vision
        cleared his throat and then said,
"That figure on this mountain
        is a story worth recountin'
Between you and me the man you see
        is the infamous 'Old Ben.'"

THE LEGEND:
Old Ben was a world-class skier
        who skied here in years long past
His old wood skis were much longer
        than the shadow that he cast

He skied this mountain eighty years
        'til the age of ninety-two
No young hot-dogger could catch him
        though so many had tried to

His love of skiing was legend
        to the throngs who skied up here
and though many tried to modernize
        his odd style and his gear
Old Ben was quite resistant to all those
        who were insistent which of course
was quite consistent
        with his independent ways

And Old Ben loved the ladies
        with a passion nonpareil
and despite his age they couldn't resist
        his ardor and his zeal
With a younger man's virility
        and startling agility
he had not outlived his ability
        up through his final days

And so it is said of dear Old Ben
        if you believe the lore
that as much as he loved skiing
        he loved the ladies more.
This story could go on and on
        but let's skip to the end
and if you're left unsatisfied well –
        maybe we'll addend.

After one long night of passion
        Old Ben looked a little ashen
but decided that a brisk ride
        down the mountain would be smart

His fair lady having gone
        he strapped his wood skis on
then took a handy sip of brandy
        to give his old ticker a jump start

Once on the hill he used his skill
        to maneuver to the top
At the height he didn't feel quite right
        but he refused to stop
It was later said he suffered
        from an episode ventricular
concurrent with a stirring
        in his area testicular

Because he grabbed his heart then grabbed
        his part and both his poles went flying
And Old Ben tumbled down the hill
        no question he was dying
In the end folks here know
        Ben went the way he'd want to go —
on his mountain still a pro
        his old wood straight up in the snow

It appears that Old Ben finished
        reputation undiminished
and no folk hero could ever
        ask for more
Amidst untold confusion
        dear Old Ben reached his conclusion
and his life has now become
        the stuff of lore."

EPILOGUE:

As was typical of him John
        entertained us on a whim

then drank his drink and with a wink
        got up and walked away
But he took care to leave behind him
        the joyful spirit that defined him
to remind us that what binds us
        is the love we give each day

****

PRAY FOR SNOW

The leader called a meeting.
The skiers knew what he would say:
"There's no snow upon our mountains;
Guys and gals: we need to pray"

So they formed a circle around him
and bowed their heads in prayer;
they ranted and they chanted
until their voices filled the air

And the sounds rose to the heavens
until they reached an icy shelf
where through spring, summer and autumn
Lady Snow slept by herself

Those earthly voices roused her
gave her shivers and she thought
To be the object of such raw desire
frankly, makes me – hot!

She dropped a few flirtatious flakes
which made nary a sound
then spread her smooth soft whiteness
She was ready to get down!

She carpeted the mountains
with layers of fine white powder
as if to say "COME GET ME, GANG"
As the excited chants grew louder!

And they skied upon the mountains
and they partied through the night
for their fervent prayers were answered
and everything was right.

******

THE SNOW DANCER

At a winter skiers' gathering
the members sighed with sadness
The weather was still summer-like
which for them gives rise to madness

Oh, they spoke of Global Warming
said "The weather's been bizarre
since it's summer in winter in the east
the west should be colder by far"

And while they were lamenting
the unfairness of their plight
unnoticed a woman slipped outside
with intent to make things right

She stepped into the darkness
of that warm November night
The sky was clear the moon was full
The stars were shining bright

In a circle of moonlight on the ground
she stood as if in trance
and began to sway and undulate
in a slow seductive dance

Her arms waved with glorious grace
like a beautiful bird in flight
as she danced for snow in the solitude
and silence of the night

When the meeting finally ended
she would deliver a gift to all:
The crowd would come out to find her
in the midst of a huge snowfall

And so it came to pass that night
as the skiers left the hall
they saw a spectral lady in white
and heavy snow began to fall.

Frustration vanished in the air
as they watched the snow descending
because the magical lady in this poem
gave them all a happy ending.

****

HAWAIIAN FANTASY

The sign said:
> *Ski Hawaii—finest powder you can find—*
> *ungroomed slopes like sugar,*
> *no lifts but worth the climb*

They call it Mauna Kea
White Mountain by translation
Highest skiing in the world
A truly unique vacation

Now I'm no skier everyone knows
but I'm going to try because geez
it's warm here and I've been told
they wear bikinis with their skis

There's a sudden growl and rumble
Yikes, I think I've made an error
My nerves begin to quiver
and my heart is filled with terror

The ground begins to vibrate
As I stand here at the crown
I'm suddenly shoved forward
racing scalding lava down

All my prior research
Said this volcano is inert
I thankfully reach the bottom
still upright and unhurt

This insane experience
took quite some time to dispel
It was just a dream, a nightmare
but like hot flashes from hell

I'm a fan of warmer weather
and in fairness you should know
that this nightmare was my reward
when for you skiers I prayed for snow

****

WINTER MISTRESS

As memories of summer fade
winter's chill pervades the air.
Leaves have fallen flowers are gone
the landscape is left bare.

We pray for nature's artistry
to redecorate the scene when
from high above our earthly realm
comes the bountiful White Queen.

She glistens in the sunlight
gives the night an ethereal glow
as on crystal wings she floats to earth
Her Majesty, Queen Snow

She drapes herself upon the trees
reclines upon the hills
in silent invitation to all
who come to test their skills.

They stand tense upon the precipice
a tingling in their nerves
as they contemplate her beauty
and the danger of her curves.

Her softness spread across the land
she beckons all to come and play.
Will they yield to her or she to them
and let them have their way?

A masterful seductress
she will titillate and tease
but demands respect at every turn
lest she bring them to their knees.

If they comply, not being shy
she will thrill them to their core;
then come spring this clever mistress
will leave them wanting more.

******

THE WORLD

UNCHAINED

I slipped a note into a crack
in the Western Wall which
perhaps no one will ever see
Should someone chance to find it
he won't know it came from me

I wrote about my anguish
at all that had been lost—
the friends and family ripped away
in the years of the holocaust

The pain of those memories lives on
even after all these years
and while time has somewhat healed
those wounds, they still bring me to tears

I'm not interned as my ancestors were
though the horror still remains
I take pride in the strength of those
whose blood flows through my veins

But I cannot forever relive a past
which by fortune was not mine
and instead embrace the progress made
though it's taken too much time

I'm grateful to be alive and free
of those ancient ties that bind
My heart beats a rhythm of freedom
and is my chosen state of mind

****

EMPTY PLAYGROUND

The New Orleans tour bus full
of tired travelers rumbles down
a rain-soaked street past a school
where umbrella-wielding parents
line the sidewalk waiting to protect
their progeny from the downpour.

The bumping and rocking of the bus
lulls me into nostalgia when it comes
to a stop beside an empty playground,
and I'm reminded of a similar stop
on another rainy-day bus ride years ago
while visiting a place where we had fought
a senseless war.

Tears erupt from my eyes as I recall
how rain-soaked swings swayed,
teeter-totters bobbed up and down
ghostlike in the wind and it seemed
I could hear the voices of children
who never got to play there
in the squeak of wet rusty hinges.

As the bus begins to move again
I'm back in the present returning
from an old plantation where costumed
actors recreated a joyful 1800s garden party
and I wonder if I will forevermore
be moved to tears by the sight
of an empty playground in the rain.

****

RED RIDING HOOD

We chatted amicably, she and I
and when her mate arrived
she asked if he and I were acquainted

> "We are," he said, "for many years
> though we don't know each other well.
> We met in Viet Nam."

He turned to me then and asked,

> "Were you a Green Beret?"

> "Oh, no; I was a Red Riding Hood."

He nodded,

> "Ahhh, after the fray.
> And as such, what did
> you find?"

> "A lone wolf," I replied,
> "Frenzied and exhausted but
> not asleep; its eyes searched
> for its mate . . . you know,
> a wolf alone does not rest."

****

I HEAR VOICES
[a message of solidarity with the students of
Marjory Stoneman Douglas High School]

I
I hear
I hear voices
I hear voices of children
I hear voices of children laughing,
I hear voices of children laughing, screaming,
I hear voices of children screaming, crying
I hear voices of children crying, praying
I hear voices of children praying, dying
I hear voices of children praying, mourning

I
I hear
I hear voices
I hear voices of children
I hear voices of children mourning,
I hear voices of children mourning, praying,
I hear voices of children praying, marching
I hear voices of children, marching, speaking
I hear voices of children speaking, trying

I hear their voices, the children—
    marching, speaking, trying—

    to make a difference.

       LISTEN.

****

They flee from their homes
We fight to keep them from ours
Bugs and foreigners

IMAGINE A LAND

Imagine a land
where freemen roam
where earth and sea
alike are home
Where peace flows free
as air and mist
And brotherhood
with all exists

All races and creeds
walk side by side
with complete respect
for each other's pride
There's neither hunger
nor despair
but love and food
for all to share

No greed nor hate
for any man
Each pulls his weight
as best he can
No war, no need
for military
Dissension solved
by commentary

But alas it's proved
beyond a doubt
neither man nor beast
can live without
their need to show
superiority
over perceived
inferiority

So here we spin
in the universe
trying to improve
but getting worse
because our species
can't agree
on a world that
values unity

Greed and power
won't get us far
Just take a look at
where we are

In the future our "progress"
will have one distinction
it will have progressed us
into early extinction

****

MAYBE IF I KNEW YOU BETTER

We are not from different worlds
simply disparate places
with different histories, beliefs

We may not look precisely alike
but we are of the same genus
life flows red through our veins

So, tell me of the place of your birth
Introduce me to your progenitors
their struggles, victories, ideals

Trust me with your memories
your pleasures, your pain
Tell me why you hurt
so I may know how to soothe you
and provide the sustenance you need

Share with me your secret dreams
that I may experience your life
in my imagination as my own
and understand our diversity

When you are with me in body
yet your mind wanders
take me to the place you go
that I may walk there with you

Do this and I will the same
I will know your life and you, mine
And perhaps we may live together in peace

******

ON THE DEATH OF A TERRORIST
May 2, 2011

The airwaves crackle with sound
as TV stations around the world harmonize
in a near-deafening multi-lingual chorus
of what approximates "The Witch is Dead."
And oh, the jubilation, the phone calls—
"Have you heard? The Witch is dead.
The Dragon is slain."

I listen, I hear, but I don't understand.
Where are my ruby slippers? I must
find my ruby slippers so I can feel
what they feel, so I can click my heels
together and go back to the fantasy
of the way things should be.

A gigantic green creature, perched on a rock
takes a hit from a glass pipe, asks me
who I am and suddenly I don't know.
But, wait. Now I remember:

I'm Alice and my ruby slippers are gone,
buried under the rubble of the Twin Towers,
those towering testaments to the triumph
of American testosterone.

Buried, along with the remains of mothers
and fathers, sons and daughters,
grandparents and all the unfinished lives
that tried to make the world a better place
for their own in whatever way they could.

The politicos claim: "Justice has been
served." "A victory for democracy."
A voice of reason asks: "How many
are taking credit for destroying the beast?
How many have a clear conscience and
had no part in creating the monster in
the first place?"

Am I in Mudville? This must be Mudville
because there is no joy here today.

****

WE MUST

Life keeps moving
faster and faster
Every day seems
to bring new disaster:
earthquakes, tsunamis,
tornadoes and more
flatten the landscape,
restructure the shore

People on streets
and in cars with guns
kill with bullets
and hit and runs
Rockets and spy drones
are under construction
and more ominous weapons
of mass destruction

Astounding advances
in military technology
enable decimation
without guilt or apology
The most brilliant minds
in the scientific community
seem bent on destruction
rather than unity

Can we teach a child
to "love his brother"
when we pit even our Gods
against each other

We must stop this inanity,
cure the insanity,
and swallow our vanity
for the sake of humanity

******

THROUGH THESE WINDOWS

Through these windows
I see chaos attempt to
make itself understood
with no apology for what
it is as our world changes
before our eyes.

Superstorms brew.
Glaciers melt.
Polar bears die.
Rivers overflow.
Mountains crumble.
Nuclear reactors leak.
Airplanes disappear
without a trace.

Young Johnnie's got a gun
and he's gone to school to kill—for fun

Progress rages on
too much, too fast.
Our humanity is lost
in its effort to keep up:
families divided,
values in disarray,
friends unrecognized.

Hunger is rampant:
for food,
for freedom,
for peace,
for connection.

Minutes fly by.
Day and night mingle
in strobe-like flashes
as the sun and moon
play tag in the sky.

The pages of history turn.
Another year vanishes.

We fear invaders from
foreign lands, blind to
the war and need which
rage in our own streets.

For now, the Philistines
have won; a new fight
for freedom has begun.

Still, the sun shines,
birds sing,
trees lift leafy limbs,
flowers turn fragile faces
to the light, and somehow
hope still smiles
through painful tears.

A courageous few gather
to feed the hungry,
welcome the displaced,
hold hands of the needy
to create balance in
a tilted world

Look in through these windows
at the world within these
withering walls, not so different
from the world outside.

Here too is chaos and hunger
but also love and compassion
burning like the sun.

Look inside for the light.

****

ENOUGH ALREADY

Gun violence has escalated
The crime rate is intense
committed by both citizens
and those charged with our defense.

So much chaos in our streets
seclusion a small part of why
Anger, bigotry, and suppression
have emotions running high.

Much as we try to stop them
these feelings just go on
We must do more to bolster
those unfairly put upon.

Frustration is easy to understand
though its expression is often blurred
by the volume and fury in which it's framed
in the effort to be heard.

Hate speech doesn't make a dent
in what should truly be desired—
to see differences between us
as qualities to be admired.

We must stop the trend to color-code
every human interaction
which only serves to propagate
a greater chain reaction.

Can we use kinder, gentler words
that touch the soul and heart
instead of loud and bitter words
which tear us further apart.

If we speak love instead of hate
so much could be forgiven
and this world would surely be
a place we'd all be proud to live in.

****

MY COUNTRY, 'TIS OF THEE
July 20, 2019.

I sit in the dark and stare
at the yellowish sliver of moon
visible through my window.

Fifty years have passed
and I sometimes wonder
if any of it is true—
the whole Neil Armstrong
walk on the moon thing,
planting the flag, and saying
those memorable words.

And if it is true, were those
very words scripted
for the moment if or when
that first step was taken
on the moon's surface.

Oh, they were good words,
clever, though we have yet to see
that true giant step for anything
but a few egos.

In the year 2001 America
was vandalized by terrorists from afar.
We wondered when, not if,
it would happen next.

In the years since then, it has
happened again and again and again;
unfortunately, countless times,
not only by foreign terrorists
but by homegrown ones.

Carefree lives were shattered,
personal security destroyed
and we wonder every day when,
not if, it will happen again.

America, if you really want to take
that giant step for mankind,
take away the guns, feed your hungry;
shelter your homeless and freedom seekers.
Care for your sick even if they can't pay.

Take care of your people!
It's time to be the great country
you claim to be.

Is that too difficult?
Well, perhaps it _is_ easier to go to the moon.

****

London, Paris, Brussels, Nice, Istanbul,
Barcelona, Boston, Orlando, New York City,
San Antonio, Parkland, ...

WHO ARE YOU

In moments everything changed
the ocean slowed its tides
the sun dulled,
the beautiful became pallid
as if all of life had drained away.
The world lost its laughter
and we cried.

You rushed into the nightclub,
the street, airport, train, school, church,
clothed with weapons and bombs
as with wild eyes, you scanned the scene
and carried out your plan.

Did you hate, did you fear?
Did you?

When you violated each venue,
shot your weapon,
pressed the button on your bomb,
stepped on the accelerator of your car,
was your purpose clear?

What thoughts were in your head?
Did you believe you would get out alive
when everyone else was dead.

Were your countrymen there?
Were you aware? Did you care?

Now you're gone too.
No one is proud of you,
No praise will be bestowed.
You are not a hero.
There is no reward.

****

THE FIELDS OF EDEN

First there was a tiny seed
then another and another
until the garden was filled
with all manner of life
growing and thriving together.

In time toxic weeds appeared
which by guise and gloss
overpowered and destroyed
greedy for space
unwilling to live in harmony
with existing life forms.

The most vibrant and sturdy
inhabitants of the garden
attempted to seduce
the wanton weeds
meld with them to diminish
their ability to threaten
health and survival of all.

Despite every effort
discord and degradation prevailed.
The beautiful were diminished.
The marauders wreaked mayhem
decimated the divine intention
that Earth was to be the garden.

Instead, the Fields of Eden
slowly withered to dust

****

BEYOND THE HORIZON

I want to believe there is a place
beyond the horizon where sky, sea,
mountains and sand converge
and those who have left this plane
are welcomed by loving gods
and goddesses to live among them
and dance together in the sun
and beneath the stars
to mystical music of the wind
and song of the surf
and all earthly dreams
unrealized are fulfilled

where days are bright and alive
with orange fire of the sun
and, when need be, knowing clouds
bring crystal droplets of liquid life
to quench all that thirsts for renewal
in every realm of creation.

I want to believe that in the fullness
of this existence, as the passing soul of time
swells with the deepening colors of the sky
all our lost ones will conspire with the gods
to heal all that ails this world for those left behind
and for others who will follow and when
one day all are reunited in this great beyond
all will be honored equally.

I want to believe.

****

PERHAPS TOMORROW

Dust motes float
in beams of sunlight
near my kitchen window
a tiny living galaxy
visible only in this spot
at this hour in the light of day.

Thousands of minuscule planets
hang in the air ready
to dispatch minute life forms
beyond human vision and also
beyond human comprehension.
They will set the world to right.

What is overabundant will
disappear forever—hunger,
hostility, greed, and be replaced
by what is most lacking—
equality, compassion, communion.

A cloud passes over the sun
and steals the light.
The galaxy disappears.
Nothing is changed today.

Perhaps tomorrow.

****

CHEFCHAOUEN
[Blue City of Morocco]

Oh, how it glows in the morning sun
a jewel of cobalt and indigo
like the wonder of God's sky.

Chefchaouen, first a fortress against
the Portuguese, then a haven
for we refugees—Jews, Moors, conversos
who fled our homes in Spain when
the Inquisition threatened to destroy
all who did not adhere to the zealots'
religious ideals.

We found passage across the Strait
of Gibraltar, made our way into unfamiliar
territory, and built our humble homes,
hidden in narrow passageways, behind
rocky shields, safe in the folds
of the magnificent Rif Mountains.

And when we were finished, we painted
all of it blue—every wall, every building,
every step—all shades of blue,
to remind us of the sky and the God
who delivered us safe from harm.

More than five hundred years have passed
and as I look down upon it now, I see
all the different peoples who were so united
in their cause live here still, together in peace
which gives me hope for the world.

Though some of the Jews have gone to Israel,
many remain, free to be in their own way,
along with the conversos, Berbers, and Muslims
for whom the call to prayer rings out
five times each day from the mosque
on the mountaintop.

Yes, the true magic of this city lives on
despite the bustle of tourists who
will never fully comprehend the plight
of the proud people who built it, who
arrived and remain here as one.

Oh, how it glows beneath the fiery sunset,
my beautiful blue city, cobalt and indigo
buildings framed by sienna mountains
against an impossibly blue sky.

Chefchaouen, city of salvation . . . my home.

******

KAUAI

My dear friend. as you lay
recovering in your bed,
close your eyes, and I will
take you on a virtual journey
through the hidden beauty
of the Island of Kauai.

Sit behind me in a kayak
as we paddle down
the beautiful Wailua River
past dense fern grottos
and groves of coconut palms
where red-headed cardinals
and white egrets sing
with the joy of freedom
as they fly from tree to tree.

The banks are bright yellow
with sea hibiscus which
overnight turn red and fall
into the water; the blossoms
float alongside us on gentle
current as we make our way
downriver where we will
bank the kayak in a cove
and walk across the narrows
to the other side.

There we will walk through
a fern grotto, past walking
trees whose roots, like legs,
move them toward the water
and past banyan vines

which wind like serpents
up the trunks of young trees
in search of the sun's light.
Later we will return to the river,
slide down the bank, retrieve the kayak,
and make our way home to our hotel.

We will paddle upriver, and though
we may struggle against the current,
we leave this paradise in peace.

****

DAY & NIGHT

MORNING

You are the smile that tempts
one from the shadows of night
inspires a desire to dance
in the bright of your light

You are the music of the wind
which soars over the sea
the voice of love and madness
between peace and insanity

You create an enchantment
one might only dream of
those graced by your touch
shall exude only love

You excite and entrance
deliver peace with your glow
greet happy or troubled hearts
are the home all are blessed to know

****

MONDAY MORNING

I've never taken issue
with Mother Nature's perfect ways

The way she turns days into nights
then back again to days

But I request that she slow down
and perhaps sometimes forget

To turn to Monday morning
when I'm not done with Sunday yet

******

ENTRY IN A YOUNG GODDESS'S JOURNAL
ON THE MORNING OF THE SUMMER SOLSTICE

Sparkling rays of sunlight
through clusters of leaves
tease my eyes open as I lie
curled in the pocket of a triad
of branches high in an oak tree.

I stay quiet for a few moments
and allow myself a long luxurious
stretch as I try to recall what I am
to do on this beautiful summer day.
I see in the distance what appears
a shadow heading in my direction.

I tilt my head and watch curiously
as a flock of bright red finches
comes close, circles then lands
on limbs all around me to deliver
a sweet sparkling serenade
in nature's own surround sound.

They remind me that today
is the summer solstice and it is I
who must go to greet the goddesses.
There is much to do to mitigate
the mess mortals have made
of humanity and of this beautiful planet.
Some humans, claim it is their gods
who direct them—their all-knowing
compassionate benevolent and loving gods.

I know of no gods—and I've known many
who would deign to destroy such perfection
but I am not mortal. I may not judge.

Of course, great Olympians like Zeus
bring the thunder when necessary
but then his cute son, Apollo,
brings back the sun; and even
that hunky Roman, Mercury, who is—
well . . . mercurial, is no destroyer.
He's tough and tender and oh so . . . sexy.

Ahh but that's a story for another day.
Now I must go—lest the greater goddesses
grow impatient

******

NIGHT

There's a sinister stillness to this night.
The air hangs heavy, clings like a sticky film;
even its cool makes a body sweat.
What is visible of the sky is black as coal.
Thick gray clouds create eerie light.

Cathedral spires of cypress trees,
dark silhouettes against the clouds,
are poised like rockets ready to launch.
Motionless, they stand tense
with not even the tiniest sway.

Mother Nature has inhaled all breathable air,
holds it deep in her chest, reluctant to exhale.
With a flash of light and a distant
low growl of thunder, her old friend Zeus
reminds her he is willing to serve.

But she is not angry tonight, only sad,
and her tears fall gently, steadily through
night and into morning until her well runs dry.
Apollo, proud son of Zeus, always ready
in his chariot of gold, brings back the sun

****

NOIR NIGHT

moonbeams
stealthy as Ninjas
slide through slats in shutters—
unheard

slender silver fingers
probe velvet silence
slip smoothly
into dreamer's dream

where in solitude of dark
silver silhouetted lovers
dance in moonlit haze
entwined in loving embrace

sudden night noises
screech of brakes
crack of backfire
alter dreamer's dream

one silver silhouette backs away
points pistol—spray of silver
second silhouette slowly
dissolves into darkness
moonbeams slide stealthily back
through slats in shutters
deserting disrupted dream
disturbed dreamer screams

heedless night melts into dawn.

****

INSOMNIA

Listen to the silence stark and chill
as a starless sky in the dead of night
Thoughts churn against your will
silently thunder behind your sight

As a starless sky in the dead of night
stealthy shadows beseech the dawn
and silently thunder behind your sight
as darkness meets the waiting morn

Stealthy shadows beseech the dawn
A stillness makes the thunder slow
As darkness meets the waiting morn
light and darkness conjoin in glow

A stillness makes the thunder slow
As peace flows through the quiet mist
light and darkness conjoin in glow
By day's first light your soul is kissed

As peace flows through the quiet mist
thoughts churn against your will
By day's first light your soul is kissed
Listen to the silence stark and chill.

******

THE INSOMNIA SHOW

On the night stage eerie moonlight
filters through dark curtains
as shadows play hide and seek
on walls that creak and groan
in the non-silence of the silent night.

A muted rhythm fills the theater
da doom, da doom, da doom
penetrates the sleep-starved brain
as a steady flowing *shhhhhh* mixes
with thrashing tentacles of thoughts
tumbling wildly in the dark/light.

Eyes close to shut out shadows,
dull all sounds, then open to wicked
light of turbulent wakefulness
as the unticking clock on the nightstand
screams its message in green LED
beams: *4:00 a.m. - little time left for
dreams.*

Silent prayers: *Oh, Hypnos, God of
sleep, spirit me away, weightless
and willing to your cave palace
where dreams are made.*

A breeze ruffles the curtains with
the flutter of godlike wings.

Peace envelops like a gentle mist.
A slow roll into dream begins when
from the depths of silence comes once
more the muted rhythm and *shhhhhh*
from an unfathomable somewhere.

In the limbo of this near sleep/near dream
you search for the origin of those sounds,
now coming faster, louder. Eyes open wide,
scan the room. The sound is everywhere—
in the yard, the walls, your ears, chest.

Your pounding heart finally slows as dawn
with its gray light quietly takes the stage
to announce the day and at last, seduced
into sleep, you float gently away to a place
of joy and laughter, soft music—and the
unwelcome *beep beep beep* of the alarm clock.

****

AND NOW THE NIGHT

And now the night is done
dreams have been dreamed
stars have retreated
   to their heavenly homes

As a new day is born
shadows of something missed
linger in the room
   cast by light through shades

Daylight's arrival ignites
flashes of somnambulant adventures
real or imagined
   which confound the wakened brain

A scent, lost in memory,
hangs like a fog in the room,
a predator of dreams past, present
   blends with breeze from window

This invasion of dawning light,
flashing specters of illusions
and hint of unknown familiar
   challenge images in the mind

Had they lasted longer—dream,
night, truth—all would be whole
instead of finely veiled fragments
   of dubious nocturnal exploits

The quest for comprehension persists
even as the mystic memories fade
to where remnants of dreams
   conjoin to create another

In the fullness of new day,
the flurry of relentless activity
displaces the haunting conundrum
  which languishes behind the eyes

And now the night comes anew
with recreated dreams which once more
slip into the slumbering psyche's
  fantasies—frivolous or unfathomable

****

CHASING A DREAM

It clings like a shadow
but more distinct
then disappears
during the ascent
to consciousness
a moment in time
utterly un-remembered
but for awareness
that there had been
something which
now begs to be recalled.

In the dull quiet of morning,
red dervishes, silver comets,
dance behind closed eyes
as slowly an inner sight
sometimes acquired in meditation
or deep concentration begins
to recognize vague shapes
and the dream reappears
but incomplete.

The concentration needed
to make connection is elusive
and the dream slips further
and further away until it fades
into nothingness once more.

Frustrated attempts to return
to sleep bring hyper-awareness
of weight of blanket draped
across legs, night sounds audible
only when sleep won't come:

drip of faucet two rooms away
creaks of walls, and shudder of pane
when wind touches window.

At long last, peace prevails
Color again fills the inner sight
with a visual feast and for an
instant the dream is back,
just as the black veil of sleep
descends to drape it in darkness
and delete it forever from memory.

****

SUSPENDED

Trapped in an impenetrable
veil of silence, suspended
in a deep abyss alone
eyes open but unseeing
I float paralyzed and terrified.

Thoughts grope wildly for
something, anything familiar
when a sudden burning tingling
touches my fingertips and slithers
hot all through my limbs.

A scream, mine, pierces the
silence as the slow escalator
from dream to wakefulness
ascends and reveals dark
silhouettes to tease my blind
eyes which now open to light
and I am once more in my bed,
warm, whole, alive.

I breathe past my pounding
heart, touch the clock on the
nightstand to reassure myself
I'm really here,
then return to sleep.

****

WHEN WE SLEEP

After midnight in the darkest hours
    when all the world's asleep
and we've surrendered all our powers
    to wander in the deep
expanse beyond our senses
    unaware of what we'll find
devoid of all defenses
    as we leave this realm behind,

do we still have ability
    to know what's dream or real
or have we lost facility
    to interpret what we feel?
What were the last thoughts in our minds
    before we reached the void?
Would those thoughts now be defined
    as food for thought for Freud?

What if beings from distant stars
    stealthily abduct us
and on return our boudoirs
    we find that they have shucked us
of the hardened shells of shattered goals
    we hide beneath our pride
to reveal our pure but tattered souls
    buried deep inside.

Are our actions weighed and measured
    and by mythic gods reviewed
and then solely for their pleasure
    are we with their ideals imbued?
Oh, merciful gods, don't grieve us
    with your other-worldly test
but leave us in the protective arms
    of Morpheus to rest.

****

THE LIGHT
&
THE DARK

CRICKETS

During a recent stay in Mexico
I heard sweet music soft and low.
From where it came, I couldn't tell—
I was alone in my motel.

Though slightly muffled I could detect
a resonance like an echo effect.
I stepped out the door and looked around
but saw not a soul, heard not a sound.

Back inside I looked everywhere
for I still heard voices from somewhere.
I stood on my toes, bent down on my knees
searching for those sweet harmonies.

Then I thought *perhaps the bath*
and though the suggestion made me laugh,
I wandered in there just to see
and what I saw flabbergasted me;

for right there on the bathtub floor were
three brown crickets and a black one—four.
They sang so sweetly and so carefree;
that is . . . until they noticed me.

I couldn't believe my ears and eyes
when one said: "Ay caramba! We're busted, guys"
Of course, this made my poor brain balk
but still I asked, "You guys can talk?"

And with accents from south of the border
they introduced themselves in short order:
"I'm Juan, I'm Pablo, I'm Jorge said three;" the
Fourth said: "the Gringo—from New York, that's me."

My head was spinning; that's a fact.
This could be a million-dollar act.
And as I sat, an idea unfurled—
I could present them to the world.

An act that's so unique as this
would be a sensation; it couldn't miss.
But what could I offer to possibly tempt them?
Their short life span might pre-empt them.

Food and shelter? They could find those
and they don't need money or fancy clothes.
I shook my head. I sat and stared
at those four crickets who looked so scared.

What was I thinking? That was just wrong—
I've lived in Hollywood much too long.
But perhaps a place where they'd feel safe
from birds and bees and even snakes.

With fruit & leaves for food & shelter,
a cool place away from the summer swelter.
They could make sweet music all day long
and no threats would interrupt their song.

Oh, their lives would be so great
they might be tempted to procreate.
They could make music all the time;
that would be magical, sublime.

They were just little crickets after all.
Fame would mean nothing to them at all.
Forget exploitation . . . I had no regrets—
I decided to take them home as pets.

******

AS IS—NO WARRANTY

In big black bold block letters
the signs, each hung from a
blue ribbon, virtually screamed:

AS IS—NO WARRANTY

Attached to each was a full page
of comments in what appeared
to be personally handwritten script.

One stated:
"Sleek, shiny little number, solid
bumper, all original parts." And
in parenthesis, "If it looks this good
now, imagine it in its prime."

Another, "Thoroughly inspected
inside and out, great shape—
like new (almost); a little quirky,
normal wear and tear but incredibly
cozy and comfortable."

I roamed around the lot randomly
reading the signs, fascinated by this
unique mode of advertising. Not all
complimentary, the comments all
sounded so sincere.

One said, "Slow to start but still has
get up and go." Another, "Don't judge
a book by its cover, this coupe's
a contender."

I returned to the first one, looked it over,
carefully perused the page again
and thought: This is the one I want.
I looked around; no one was nearby
so, I picked up the sign by the blue
ribbon, placed it purposefully around
my neck and sauntered down the street.

 It was perfect, it was me:

     AS IS—NO WARRANTY

****

THE TOO UPTIGHT TO MEDITATE MEDITATION

The leader says:
"Sit comfortably, close your eyes.
Concentrate on your breathing.
Inhale to the count of four.
Exhale as you count to four once more.
Enter the realm of relaxation.
Clear all clutter and agitation."

>   *I try to inhale to the count of four*
>   *and wonder what I'm doing this for.*
>   *My body's tense with angst and fear;*
>   *there's no damned realm of relaxation here.*

He says:
"Create your own special hideaway
a place of peace, comfort, calm.
It may be a room, a beach, a park.
Note every detail of how it should be—
the color, decor, the air around you.
See yourself there. Let its beauty surround you."

>   *My heart and pulse are in a race.*
>   *I mentally run to find such a place*
>   *through fields of tall and brittle grass.*
>   *And twice I trip and fall flat on my . . ..*

He says:
"Inhale the scent of where you are.
Continue to concentrate on your breath.
Feel your body relax from head to toe.
The tension dissipates with every
exhale. Your arms and legs are limp and weighted.
Your eyelids are heavy as if you're sedated."

He says:
"Let everything go you're almost there.
You're floating, weightless, light as air.
The world around you has fallen away.
You hear only my voice and what I say.
Positive thoughts come steadily.
You are the master of your destiny."

****

BALD

No apologies should be made
by members of the male population
who choose to boldly broadcast
their baldness rather than wear
cartoonish comb-overs
terrible toupees
or wooly watch caps
to nurture newly seeded segments
of their naked noggins.

Bald is beautiful
bare is brave, ballsy.
It screams spontaneous,
secure, sexy.
So, guys—feel free
to shear and shave
(though that's not *bona fide* bald).
Someday, somewhere
some lusty lady will
be dazzled and delighted
by your denuded dome.

****

BOOKED

The cops booked me on trumped-up charges.
"Indecent exposure," the *gendarme* said.
And even though I was fully clothed
he just couldn't get it through his head
that sharing champagne and caviar
with poor folks at a cheap restaurant
might constitute "exposure"—to something new,
by a well-intentioned *bon vivant.*

Instead, he had the nerve to say
I shared my wares with abandon
as if my heartfelt beneficence
had any intent to hurt someone.

Now it may be true this luxurious fare
was not quite bought and paid for
but using it to inspire some *joie de vivre*
is what the stuff was made for.

I'm charged with a crime I didn't commit
but my attorney says I'll walk.
And as for the crime they overlooked,
well, "I'll be damned before I'll talk."

****

THE BURNING BUSH
A twisted look at the Good Book

Moses heard the voice of God
in a burning bush;
he had an epiphany,
gained knowledge and insight.
He took two tablets—possibly more.
Did he call God in the morning?
Perhaps.

Years ago, I heard music
in a way I never had before.
There wasn't exactly a burning bush
unless you consider
sitting in the nosebleed seats
at the Forum during a Bob Dylan concert
inhaling the smoke of a thousand sprigs
of burning cannabis, a burning bush.
Close enough.

It wasn't only the music;
it was the lyrics,
the people around me,
the total focus on this young man
who our parents' generation
was writing off as a drug addict,
singing his heart out
with the insight of a sage

In one song he asks not only
how often one has to look up
before seeing the sky and how long
one must listen before hearing
people cry and then, how many people
need to die before it's clear there
have been too many.

So what do you think? Are these the
ruminations of a bum, a drug addict?

Ok - back to Moses:

Upon the sacred mountaintop
walked Moses long ago
tending to his meager flock
what awaited he couldn't know.
Suddenly to his nose, there came
a scent of something burning.
He followed the scent, unaware
of what he'd soon be learning.
He found a solitary bush
engulfed fully in flame;
from it came the voice of God
who called Moses by name.

It was after this that Moses left
and guided by God's hand
he led his people from Egypt
in search of the promised land.
But the people tired of walking;
they were angry and felt lost;
they indulged in drunken orgies
ignorant of the cost.

And Moses climbed the mount again,
barefoot, tired, ashamed;
wondering if he'd angered God
and feared he would be blamed.
For three long months he stayed away,
exhausted, alone, and blue,

his people having lost their faith;
he didn't know what to do.

They worshipped idols, ignored the rules,
blasphemed in every way,
unconscious of the length of time
Moses had been away.
He returned with "God's Commandments;"
for salvation he was yearning.
But had he really heard the voice of God?
Just what kind of bush was burning?

******

COFFEE FOR WINE
(The Morning After Poem)

Oh to taste that first cup of coffee
    After a night of revelry divine—
Of dining and dancing and corner romancing
    And wine, yes, the ruby red wine.

Oh the scent as it floats down the hallway
    Is the rooster announcing the sun
To a brain in decline from the ruby red wine
    But I'd drink it again for the fun.

Oh hear it drip-drip through the filter
    Filled with lovely ground French roasted beans.
If it weren't for the wine, I'd get to it just fine
    But my legs tell me: "Find other means."

Oh bless the solid walls that now guide me
    As I follow the scent of dark roast.
Next time I'll decline the ruby red wine
    But right now I need coffee and toast.

Oh auto drip pot on the counter
    Gurgling and sputtering my name
I'd respond gleefully if only I could see
    But the wine's left me blind and quite lame.

Oh Lord, put a mug in my hand now
    And if you help me in filling it too,
There'll be no more dining with ruby red wining
    I shall stick with my French-roasted brew.

****

MY COMPUTER THINKS IT'S PSYCHIC

Something about my computer
     has become very concerning.
Technologically I'm kind of slow
     although I am still learning.
But the messages I've received
     from my computer seem to me
of a much more personal nature
     than one might expect them to be

Your memory is full, it says
     when I'm trying to recall
the name of that funny poem
     I wrote for you last fall.
Now I know I tend to forget a lot
     since this machine's been keeping track
but does my memory being full, mean
     I can't get the old ones back?

Then it says *Your cloud is full* —
     what does it know of my cloud,
The one I walk on when I've done
     a thing that really makes me proud?
Or the one to which I'm transported
     When I meet someone I like?
It's Full? Well, there's only room for two—
     this thing can take a hike!

You have no right to do this
     it beeps when I attempt to resave
a document I've just revised.
     Why won't this thing behave?!
I've resaved stuff a thousand times
     the way I did just now.
It doesn't like my new changes
     so it's going to disallow?

Your program is not responding—
       Wait or cancel, now I'm told
Well, yes, I feel like that a lot.
       I must be getting old.
But I only have one program
       and though it may be out of date
it still works pretty well for me,
       so, thank you—I will wait

Change your battery or switch
       to outlet power, it had the nerve to say.
Now, that is WAY too personal—
 that's all I have to say!

****

I'M WAITING FOR YOU

I am voluptuous—full and rounded,
cushy curves in all the right places;
firm where I need to be, soft warm
and ever willing to engulf you
in practiced pleasure.

I delight in the feel of fine fabrics
snug on my body—silky smooth
satins, suedes, velvets, treasure touching
bare skin on my arms, legs—
holding, resting.

I become delirious in my predilection
for posterior parts, all sizes, and genders,
rotund compact fleshy or flat
pressed solidly against me.

Let me comfort and calm you.
Surrender yourself
to my seductive center.
I am here waiting to share my gifts,
assuage my avid appetite for . . . ass.

Come to me. I'm yours . . .
        your favorite . . . chair

******

OUTING CUPID

Legend tells a story
        that might possibly confuse you
though if you're happily in love
        this story might amuse you:

Cupid shot his arrow of gold
        at the Olympian god Apollo
who then fell in love with Daphne
        which love caused him untold sorrow

For Cupid, full of mischief
        decided they should never wed
So, he shot the lovely Daphne
        with an arrow made of lead

Her reaction was to run away,
        an act clearly impulsive
for she now found lovesick Apollo
        totally repulsive

Poor Apollo didn't have a clue,
        so sure they'd be united
but due to Cupid's devilry
        Apollo's love stayed unrequited

So, if you are a seeker
        of love's eternal flame
employ your own devices
        and don't play Cupid's game

Because now you know the story
        and it's clear, you must admit
Cupid can't be trusted—
        he's a spiteful little twit

******

SHAMAN

In a fitful dream there came to me
an old and feeble man dressed in rags;
he held a twisted walking stick
and stumbled along babbling to himself.

In a voice somehow familiar,
he said to me,

"There is magic in this world.
Harness it and teach it
to your children."

"SHAME, MAN," I cried,
"Only a God can do that."

Some nights later, in another dream,
a handsome stranger danced with me
and captured my heart. He was dressed
all in white and had a dazzling smile.

In the same familiar voice, he whispered
stories of great love—his for me, mine
for him, and for the children we would bring
into enlightenment. Suddenly, he was gone.

"SHAM MAN," I shouted to the night.
You are not real."

Last night in the darkness came the voices
of my children; they thanked me for their lives
and for their knowing which
came from all my rights and my wrongs.

After, there appeared a near-naked tribal elder
who spoke to me in that familiar voice
but in a tongue I could not understand.
Then he smiled and faded into dust.

"SHAMAN," I whispered.
And then I slept.

******

DAY OF THE DEAD

As the fog begins to lift
bit by bit, the murky layers
fly away into oblivion,
like ghosts dissolving
in the shadows of first light.

Tiny rays of sunshine creep
like tentative scouts
from just below the horizon
to banish the last eerie specters
of night from the glow of morning.

Yet, a sinister stillness lingers in the air
for today is the Day of the Dead
and it seems the departed
have been disturbed in the night
by a subtle shift in the earth.

Today they walk unobserved
among the living in search
of companions to dwell with them
forever in their eternal rest.

For whom have they come?
Surely not the little witches
and goblins who roamed
the darkened streets hours
before the shift.

Do they seek the workers?
The shirkers? The happy? The sad?
Perhaps it's the good or only the bad.
Could they want the deceivers,
or simply the true?

The answer is uncertain;
are they searching for YOU?

****

DIALOGUE WITH DEATH

I once had a dialogue with Death.
At first, I was tremulous, terrified;
but death spoke to me sincerely
in a voice like deep blue velvet.
It commanded me to listen;
its intensity made me hear.

It said: "I am never far away;
I am all around, just like life.

Don't be afraid; just live . . . as I do"

****

NO LIGHT

Deep in a forgotten wood
sits a dark and shadowed shack
where neither light nor laughter dwell
its walls grizzled and black

Therein dwells a tortured soul
immersed in such despair
that not passion, purpose, or desire
can find an entry there

What anguish leads to such a place
of dismal, desolate ground
where only whispers in the wind
break the silence all around

What transgressions alleged or true
might haunt a soul so much
as to exile one to spend a life
devoid of human touch

To dwell in virtual darkness
shadows the only guests
in fear the slightest light of life
stir longing in the breast

Should you come upon these woods
though trees and flowers may court you
take note the rocks and mottled leaves
left in the path to thwart you

And if you near the shadowed shack
be aware as you begin
that if your heart weighs heavy
you just might be sucked in.

****

VIGILANTE

In a now-defunct genre of magazine, called a horror comic book, though in truth there was nothing remotely comical involved, there once appeared a fully illustrated story of a mysterious dark-haired, woman who seduced handsome men to her home where for hours she made passionate love to them, and afterward playfully tied them to her bed creating a silken web around them as she slowly morphed into a giant black widow spider, then hovered high above the bed and prepared to feast on her terrified prey.

This was a most harrowing tale for an impressionable teenager to read.

So long suppressed in memory, it was a shock to be suddenly reminded recently, in the middle of the night, as I wandered in the dark through my house en route to the kitchen for a drink of water.

Dim light from a street lamp in the alley behind the house filtered through the curtains, creating a shadow on the den wall which made my heart pound and my breath catch in my throat. A huge spider hung on a thread from the ceiling about midway to the floor.

Aware these nocturnal creatures can be dangerous and will hide from light, I dared not cause it to flee; on second look, I was somewhat relieved to note it was not nearly as big as its shadow.

Cautiously, I stepped a bit closer, close enough to see it was black—shiny black—patent leather shiny black. There was no need to look for a bright red hourglass on her belly; we both knew what she was, but, clearly, to me, there was only room in this house for one of us.

She had to go.

But how? I weighed my options: Trap her in a paper bag? Too risky. Smash her? Not possible; she was too far from the wall. Shotgun? Messy—and I might miss. Vacuum cleaner—the only viable option.

With no choice but to leave her dangling, I hauled the vacuum cleaner from the hall closet, plugged it in, attached the long wand, and flipped the switch, then headed back to the den, the contraption at my back while holding that four-foot-long wand in front as if it were Excalibur. I pointed it at that abhorrent arachnid and sucked her in—I sucked her in for a full ten minutes, terrified she would somehow survive and retaliate.

Finally satisfied, I wheeled the vacuum cleaner outside, dislodged the dust bag, and sealed it in the trash container for pickup. Back inside, I roamed from room to room, looking in the dim light for anything that moved before I dared to turn on a light. I made coffee and turned on the TV, hoping for a late-night/early-morning comedy. Sleep that night was no longer an option.

My sleep habits have changed since then
My days are spent asleep
I sit vigils in the dark of night
When the widows choose to creep
So, friends, feel free to call me
any hour of the night
I'm right here, shotgun on my left
Trusty vacuum on my right

****

THE CLIFF

A man and a woman stand
        hearts pounding
 at the edge
        of a rocky cliff

                between two seas,

They watch the tides
        oppose one another
one blue, calm
        one dark, turbulent.

Above them gulls soar
        silver circles in a cloudless sky
wings spread in graceful flight
        carried on the wind

which blows powerful
        first in one direction
and without warning shifts
        The birds follow its whim

then dive like arrows
        wings tucked close
straight
                down
                        toward
                                churning seas

In a flash they turn
        ascend again skyward
The man and woman
        focus on their flight

They cling to each other
        startled by the power
of a sudden squall which might
        plunge them into the depths

They retreat from the edge
        but the uncaring seas
beckon in harmony with the wind
        "Come," they say

"Swim, explore, ride
        fearlessly on our tides
Let us relieve you
        of your earthly ills

"We are hope and despair
        torment and solace
turbulence and tranquility
        but we are eternal . . . come"

The man and woman inch
        slow and tentative
to the edge once again
        hands clasped together

They listen and watch the gulls above
        the seas below
Their knees bend
        feet push hard against the ground

arms swing backward
        then forcefully forward
and for a moment . . .
        they fly!

****

NOSTALGIA

PAST PRESENT FUTURE

A low branch of a big oak waves
a slow, teasing come-hither sway.
The wind whispers: *Don't do it.*

You wouldn't have back then
but now you lean against
the branch, press hands down hard
lift yourself off the ground
and sit, feet dangling, hands now
in the air and mentally shout

    Look, Ma, no hands!

The wind wails a lifetime of admonitions:

    Don't do that
        It's dangerous
            Get down now

as you rock and bounce gently up and down
back and forth on that branch
in this tree and you smile.
The wind calms, sun warms—whispers

    You could fall

You might have back then but now
you wriggle close to the trunk
pull yourself vertical and reach
for a higher branch and climb
—up—up—higher and higher.

Your heart pounds, body pulses
as you finally reach the highest branch.
You stand tall, proud, triumphant, unafraid.
You've done it and you know without
a doubt, this is only the beginning.

****

TIME

The golden glow fades from our skin
Silver shimmers in our hair
reminders that time slips by
as we live life unaware.

But in unexpected moments
we might well glimpse time pass
as leaves fall silently from trees
and in browning of the grass.

While life's velocity has increased
our own seems to have slowed
and mountains we still hope to climb
have started to erode.

Goals once set or reached for
seem at times so magnified—
some accomplished, others not.
Which ones are amplified?

Successes, failures, lessons learned—
the lives we touch will show
just how well we've lived our own
as we approach our last plateau.

Impatient time has its own plan;
it waits for no one's schemes.
We proceed at our own pace
to fulfill our fondest dreams,

Today will soon be yesterday
and yesterday last year
and without a hint of warning
tomorrow might not appear.

****

AFTER THE CRASH

I dreamed I crashed into a wall
All my thoughts and memories
spilled out and scattered on the ground
diverse and disheveled as unbound pages
of Webster's unabridged dictionary.

Helpless to collect them all
I became abruptly aware I had carried
this mélange of mayhem for so long
a crash was inevitable.

What must be kept; what must be
discarded?

I tiptoed slowly through the montage
of mental magma and unearthed
from beneath a mound of empathy
and forgiveness a large slightly tarnished
lump of love.

I gathered that trio of treasures and stuffed
them into a pocket close to my heart.

There lay great globs of sadness, pain
and madness; reluctantly I tucked away
a modicum of each in my hip pocket
to remind me that life is not always perfect.

When I happened upon a handful of humor
I sprinkled a bit into my breast pocket
but packed the rest in with the sadness
where I knew it could make the most difference.

Much lighter I proceeded on my way.

****

THE WIZARD

He appeared daily in the public square
dressed in wizard's clothes
He chatted with the passers-by
Where he came from no one knows

He spoke about his travels
the many places he had visited
imparted advice to everyone
though often unsolicited

Information about himself
bordered on ridiculous
Yet advice that he imparted
was surprisingly meticulous

He said he'd soared above the clouds
on imagination's wings
where the universe whispered in his ear
and told him many things

He said: "Stand strong for your beliefs—
for your family, your friends
These are the inner core on which
all joy in life depends

"Of all the goals one has in life
most vital is: be true
To possess things is a lofty plan
but better is: be a good you

"Teach your children love
and laughter, poetry, and song;
for then, wherever they may go
they'll feel that they belong

"Remember: dreams and wishes
may not always reach fruition
but it is the dreamers of the world
who give life definition

"If your life were a giant puzzle
with a thousand pieces scattered
you can bet one single missing piece
was not the one that mattered."

****

CLICK

When one lives in a multiplex
doors slam at all hours of day
and night. It's all unnoticed
after a while—the doors,
the TV heard through the wall
shared with a nearly deaf neighbor,
loud music from everywhere
especially in summer, when windows
and doors remain open in homes,
and in cars that move down the street.

Most of the sounds were easily ignored
even those of my front door closing
or slamming as the kids left in a hurry.
I was rarely awakened, even on those
mornings I slept late and they left
in a noisy rush—until the summer
my son was hired as a lifeguard
at the beach.

It didn't matter that he was a strong
swimmer, and on the swim team
at school—that was swimming in a pool.
The ocean is a fierce competitor.
Powerful. Deceptive. Devious.

I recalled how as a child I once saw
a drowned man pulled from the surf
and my own father's terror when
he was unable to fight a rip tide
without assistance.

My son was excited; his mother was not.

That summer, despite what wee hour
I finally retired to bed, I was kept awake
by unceasing apprehension of that quiet
click of the carefully closed door as he left
each morning.

"Keep him safe" I chanted
to no one in particular.

****

THE BW AND ME

As I rode my tiny tricycle
with diminutive grace
my concentration was broken
the smile wiped off my face.

This was my first encounter.
I was just a child of three.
The BW appeared so suddenly
and knocked the wind from me.

I found myself upon the ground
though why I couldn't explain.
I blamed it on the BW,
tearful words spoken in vain.

I cried big alligator tears
until help was by my side;
I got a hug and admonishment—
"Be careful where you ride."

The BW has followed me
through career, friendship,
and marriage, evoking insecurity
and increasing mental baggage;

a nemesis that stopped me cold
in many an endeavor and created
challenges for me I'd not have
thought of—ever.

A New York columnist used BW
as slang for "Beautiful Wife."
Someone else recalled an employer,
The "Big Wheel" in his life.

About my own BW,
the best thing I can say
is: rock solid consistency—
may come in handy one day.

Thinking back, the times
are few that I cannot recall
plowing unexpectedly
into that old Brick Wall,

lurking ever in my space
no matter what I do
as if to say "Don't worry kid,
I'm always here for you."

****

WAITING FOR THE ICEMAN

When all she knew was reaction and sensation
she had already met the man of her dreams.
She was only five then; he, twenty years more
but to her child's eye, he was magic,
for when he smiled more light seemed
to fill the room and she was sure
she smelled spring flowers in bloom.

Twice each week he arrived, so tall
in his gray uniform, he had to duck
beneath the door frame as he carried
the big block of ice to fill the gaping mouth
of the old icebox in the kitchen.

With a dimpled grin, he ruffled her hair
with his free hand and asked:
"Where'd you get those cute dimples, Curly,"
which made her giggle and blush
bright pink with pleasure.

He held the big rusty ice tongs to his face,
one pointed prong on each cheek,
then winked and said: "I got mine from these,"
which made her giggle even more.

One day a shiny new refrigerator arrived.
Her family fairly danced with excitement.
She couldn't wait to show it to the iceman.
She waited and waited, impatient, as days
dragged by, then weeks and months
but the iceman did not return.

Ten years passed and ten more
and by then she was a grown woman
and she met and married a man,
much older than she. He was tall and thin;
He called her "Curly" and had a dimpled grin.

****

THAT SONG

I'd like to say I understood every word when I first heard the song on the radio, but I didn't; the singer had an accent and I was too young to comprehend the meaning of the words.

But the voice, which years later I came to know as a truly brilliant basso, and the melody, which washed over me like a gentle wave as I played on the floor on a rainy Saturday, touched me so deeply, I stopped and sat unmoving, mesmerized.

And as Ezio Pinza continued to sing "Some Enchanted Evening," tears began to run down my young face for no reason I could fathom. My mother entered the room and asked why I was crying and all I could say was "It's so pretty."

Years later, in my mid-teens, my parents took me to see what would be the first of many productions of <u>South Pacific</u> I would see in my lifetime. Every time that song is sung in the play, I have the same first childhood reaction, although I admit, Ezio Pinza is the only one who ever brought me to tears without the entire play introducing it, which I understood, even as a young child, was the most romantic fantasy ever conceived.

******

FRAGRANCE OF FLOWERS

Something as subtle
as an unanticipated
sweet scent of flowers
can transport one to
a place long lost in memory,
as happened one day when
a light breeze through the yard
engulfed me in the redolence
of roses and jasmine.

For a moment I was seated again
in my 2nd grade classroom
chatting and giggling with friends
when the door opened
to a faint fragrance of flowers
followed by the new teacher.

Tall and striking in a long red coat
and matching hat atop blond hair,
her face bore the warmest,
most dazzling smile I'd ever seen,
all of which caused instantaneous
cessation of all talk, the only audible
sound the intake of breath as twenty-
five captivated seven-year-olds
turned their heads to stare.

She wrote her name, Mrs. James,
on the chalkboard and told us
she had a husband and a grown daughter,
then laughed as she said she had just
become a grandma.

A grandma? Impossible!
She was nothing like my ample-bodied
wrinkled Eastern European Grandma.

Mrs. James walked from desk to desk,
to learn the name of each student
and when she reached me that day
and every day thereafter, I smelled flowers—
one day roses, another day lilacs or lilies
or gardenias.

These days, even after so many years
each time I get a whiff of the fragrance
of fresh flowers, I think of Mrs. James
in her red coat and hat, smiling
her dazzling smile, smelling like flowers.

****

THE REMAINS OF TEDDY

When I was just a tiny tot
I had a teddy bear.

    I never ever felt alone
    My Teddy was always there

He slept with me in my bed
He watched me learn to walk

    He listened to my every word
    when I began to talk
He was my constant companion
through all the travails of growing

    He never judged or criticized
    even when my "bad" was showing

And when I was a teenager
at times I treated him badly—

    ignored him as if he wasn't there
    He simply sat there sadly

I think he knew I loved him
more than I'd ever say

    because folks might laugh at a teenager
    who acted out that way

Now I'm long grown and he's still here
I see him every day

    Teddy's a whole lot worse for wear
    but I won't throw him away

His legs are torn, one arm is gone,
and I mourn his missing head

      I imagine the wisdom it held inside,
      all the things he never said

So, Teddy, I can tell you now
you were always my best friend

      and though we both may fall apart
      we'll be together 'til the end.

****

GREENWICH VILLAGE

In the dim light of a dark dank basement coffee house, with black walls and a cracked stone floor, I, still a teenager, sat with friends, at a wobbly wooden table on hard uncomfortable straight-backed chairs, drinking coffee, trying to look like we belonged there among the unshaven, long-haired men and beautiful bohemian women laughing and talking and having a wonderful time. We marveled at the group of twenty-something Israeli boys at a round table who clicked their spoons together and created musical rhythms like the sound of castanets; and were fascinated by the plethora of happy mixed-race couples, unheard of uptown in those days, as we waited for something, we didn't know what, to happen. In a moment, an older (to us), 30ish-looking guy with a thick mop of curly greasy intensely black hair and a matching scraggly beard stood up and started to speak.

He said, "I saw the best minds . . . " He continued for what seemed like an eternity; getting louder and faster and the people watched and listened intently and cheered; the Israeli boys surrounded him and began to click their spoon castanets, matching his intensity, accompanying his words with just the right rhythm and volume to enhance but not detract, and I, in my naivety, having lived, I realized years later, a very sheltered existence, didn't have a clue as to the meaning or import of his words or that I was witnessing a moment in history.

We left the coffee shop that night, not sure of what we had just witnessed, and walked through the streets of Greenwich Village listening to colored boys (as they were called back then) sing melodious doo-wop harmonies under the street lights, maybe hoping to be discovered.

It was 1958.

Over the many subsequent years, I became a fan of Allen Ginsberg, not in the same way I did for Dylan or Cohen, but fascinated in a more visceral way by his poetry, his life, his friends, what he represented. In 1994 many years after I had moved to California, a tiny notice in the Los Angeles Times, caught my eye: Alan Ginsburg was going to appear at an outdoor F-theater in Long Beach, California. Amazing. It had been several years since his name had appeared in the news. I called my friend. We planned to go.

We sat on cement steps in a little outdoor amphitheater in the center of the city and waited, surrounded by aging beatniks and hippies in their berets, faded tie-dye shirts, and moonstone jewelry. We waited an hour past the time appointed for the event to begin and when an older, bald man wearing a brown houndstooth sport coat and a necktie tentatively made his way down the stairs to the podium in the center, we were certain this man was going to announce that the event would not take place. But he picked up the microphone, sat down on a wooden stool, and without introduction or preamble, that familiar booming voice began to recite the words I had heard all those years before in that dark under-ground coffee house and once again, I heard Ginsburg, in person, recite the whole of his iconic poem "Howl," as well as a few others and he captured the same rapt attention as I remembered he did all those years ago—only this time, mine included.

Afterward, like the Pied Piper, he led the crowd to a bookstore several blocks away where he sold and autographed boxed sets of audio tapes of his work. It seemed such a contradiction of who he was but it was a long way from the 1950's. I bought those tapes for $80.

That was the first and last time I ever hung around to get an autograph and now ... what a memory it elicits.

****

FOOD FOR THOUGHT AND OTHER SENSATIONS
OR RECOLLECTIONS OF RESPLENDENT REPASTS

I'm six or seven years old at my Grandma's house in a beat-up section of the Bronx when Dad comes in with a pink bakery box from which he produces a masterpiece of confectionary wizardry—the most delicate, graceful, light, beautiful, delicious and unforgettable little 2-inch-high disc of sponge cake, piled high with wondrous, wavy, whipped cream, topped with a cherry and sitting in a crown-shaped cardboard cup and he says: "I'd like you to meet Charlotte Russe."

He holds it close to my face; I suck the cherry off the top and bite down; it explodes in my mouth like fireworks in a moonless sky. I bury my tongue in the soothing softness of the whipped cream and . . . Ohhhhhh—heaven.

On some Saturday mornings, we would stand outside a restaurant on Broadway in Manhattan and watch a man in a white apron whisk eggs in a bowl, pour them into a pan of hot butter, insert the teeth of a long-handled fork into the center, and slowly, slowly twirl and twist and lightly lift the cooking eggs until there stood in the pan a tall cone-shaped mountain of golden scrambled eggs.

I was mesmerized. Although I have tried for years to master his technique I have yet to figure out how he stood those eggs up like that.

When I became a teenager, egg mountains and even Charlotte Russe's were forgotten in the sharing of hand-tossed pizza with friends, especially at the neighborhood pizza parlor because in the window of that local hangout, as Tony tossed the dough high in the air I was frozen to the spot, totally hypnotized by the

subtle flex of every muscle in his arms and chest
through his tight white t-shirt.

I watched as he first patted a big ball of dough into
a thick round pancake just big enough to fit over the top
of his two fists, then toss it high in the air, catch it lightly
on his fists, and at the same time stretch it, toss again so
it rotated a quarter turn, then again: toss, catch, stretch,
muscles flexing, toss, catch, stretch, muscles flexing,
toss, catch, stretch, muscles flexing until that dough was
a large thin perfectly flat round of dough which fit
perfectly on a large pizza pan. He then folded the edges
to make a thick rim, painted it with olive oil, spread a
ladle full of thick red tomato sauce, and covered it all
with handfuls of shredded mozzarella cheese, and a
generous sprinkle of oregano. Oh, what a sight to see—
delicious.

And the pizza was good too.

But my fondest memory is of the hot fudge sundae
shared at sixteen years old, with my first real boyfriend.
So excited to be together, we watched the woman in the
black dress & white apron walk down the aisle of the
soda shop balancing it on a tray—a clear lily glass filled
with scoops of vanilla ice cream, a hot lava flow of thick
dark chocolate oozing down the sides, topped with a
mountain of pure white whipped cream, chocolate
sprinkles and a bright red cherry.

We dipped our spoons deep down in the glass to
get a little taste of everything and then—then he turned
to me, his face so close to mine, breath chocolate sweet
and with gentle fingertips smoothed a hair from my
cheek and his chocolate-tinged lips melted into mine.

It doesn't get any better than that!

****

THE BEACH

The waves rise and fall in undulating swirls.
I sit in the sand on this familiar expanse of beach.
This sand knows all my secrets, my past, my now.

I remember how, as children we played,
you and I—laughing, crying, growing, changing.
Only this beach does not change.

I see your blue eyes, dimpled grin, wild dark hair,
muscles of your bronzed body rippling in the sun,
as, unaware of your magnificence you run into the sea.

The waves roar reminding me they have taken you.
I shout to them, "I'm here . . . Take me too,"
as I walk to the water's edge and into the sea.

The sun is bright; icy wetness bites my ankles,
legs, hips. I dive deep into a wave.
In the turbulent darkness, I feel you near.

Your voice permeates the abyss:
It implores me: "Reach for the sun, for life."

Tossed by the current, I reach out in panic
and break the surface gasping in the sun.

****

SQUARES ON A BRONX SIDEWALK

Back in the Bronx when we were
pre-teens, we counted the cement
squares on the sidewalk on our street,
my best friend and I. She started at one
end, I at the other. There were 500 in all.

We met on the 250th square directly
in front of the house where lived the boy
she loved, as told in secret whispers
and inscribed in private diary pages.

He never knew; his eyes saw only the
girl in the house across the street who
skated in the Ice Capades, and taunted
and teased him, then ran off with his
best friend.

At the 50th square down the street lived
a man and his wife, she a holocaust survivor,
who, when her husband was at work, wore
too tight clothes and too much makeup
to greet the mail carrier and the UPS man.

Dad complained that the mail was always
late and the mailman was lazy and didn't
earn his pay. I just wondered why our
mail wasn't delivered inside the house
like it was for the holocaust lady.

Next to her house lived an orthodox Jewish
family whose eldest son blushed scarlet
at the sight of his neighbor, which raised
questions as to his temple of worship and
his definition of a religious experience.

At square 300 lived the "strange family,"
she, a tall bulky joyful redhead, and he
a short swarthy Napoleonic sort who
people said, hid questionable business
practices behind a faded curtain of piety.

When their three boys grew up, they joined
the family business; two were arrested with
their dad for fraud. The third was out of
town at the time and stayed gone. The
Mom sold the house and moved away.

At the far end of the block at square 450
lived a family with two daughters and a son
I had met only once, but will never forget.
I sent him a "get well" card when he almost
died from a ruptured appendix.

About a month later as I passed his house
he came running outside in his pajamas,
ran right up to me and kissed me on my mouth,
right there, on square 450 . . .
with the whole world watching.

****

THE TROUBLE WITH JEANS / GENES

The trouble with jeans [genes] is:
they rarely fit the way you want them to
and often it's difficult to wear them
the way you think they should be worn.
Some folks attempt to alter their jeans
[genes] which can be very costly
and afterward, they never quite fit
or feel like the old well-worn ones.

Of course, the essence of one's jeans
[genes] can be better displayed with
a lot of discipline and effort, though
in the end, the style remains the same
and the manufacturers ensure that
your own jeans [genes] will never fit
anyone quite the way they fit you.

Now, my jeans [genes] have been
in my family for countless generations
and though no one before me seemed
to have been happy with them, they
wore them for a very long time;
then, with no malice or forethought,
they passed them down to me and now,
after years, I find them perfectly comfortable.

Both my son and daughter have jeans
[genes] very much like mine and they
each wear them in a most flattering
light. Perhaps the longer your jeans
[genes] are around the more interesting
they become, or, perhaps you just learn
to love them.

******

TO GRANDMA'S HOUSE
(The Bronx circa 1960)

Through the park in gleaming sunshine
sounds of life and death all mingled—
mothers rocking squalling infants,
laughing shouting running children,
rumbling wheels of passing skaters,
bobbling mumbling sunning ancients.

Avid chess games at stone tables;
sudden gasps break concentration.
Rustling red and gold leaves falling,
crackling sweetly with each footfall.
Gentle wind-songs float on breezes
humming the fresh sweet music of life.

Reaching grandma's ancient building,
ground floor Shul 'neath her apartment.
I climb the stairs and ring the buzzer,
smell the garlic steak and French fries.
This is how she says she loves me.
So damn the roaches that share my table.

Evening comes with hugs and kisses.
She shoos me out to miss the dark.
I'm warm inside from all she gave me.
I make my way through the silent park.

******

IN A SMALL CAFÉ

In years gone by they huddled in a booth
in the back of the corner soda shop
and made plans for their life together.
Now two long-lost lovers meet once more.

She sits across the table from him
her fragile hand resting on his, the years
between them apparent in her eyes.

As her gaze rests upon his face
she relives the warmth of his embrace.
The dewy mist that fills her eyes
bespeaks a love she can't disguise.

In youth her faith had dubbed a sin
the stirrings she had felt within.
Yet she never felt a hint of shame
for the child she bore who bears his name.

She lifts her hand, strokes his cheek.
Her face says all, no need to speak.
She stands and starts to walk away.
He starts to rise . . . she bids him stay.

He follows her progress to the door
his adoring unblinking eyes glazed
as he basks in the memory of years gone by.

He treasures this last spent moment of bliss,
how she turns at the door to blow a kiss.
Young, fearful, and silent, his intent misread;
his heart cries still for words left unsaid.

The faith of his youth would not abide
his taking this girl to be his bride.
So silent benefactor he became
to the child she bore who bears his name.

If just once more he could touch her cheek
and say the words he's longed to speak.
He stands and races across the floor
and disappears through the café door.

******

RAINBOWS AND DAYDREAMS

In the magic garden of childhood
        where daydreams could come true
There were always rainbows in my
        sky and there was always a "you"

You were a gypsy pony once with a
        long and silky mane
We would race beneath the rainbows
        until the light of day would wane

Once you were a frisky puppy
        and we'd race up hills so high
Then jump and reach for rainbows
        try to pluck them from the sky

Later I dreamed of the perfect mate
        who would be my heart's desire
Who would turn sad days into happy ones
        and set my world on fire

Then you appeared, my handsome prince
        Your manner was so disarming
My days of fantasy were done
        but I still nicknamed you "Charming"

And you were a clever playful mate
        just as I hoped you would be
You thrilled and filled my heart with joy
        but were elusive as you could be

A rainbow is still a stunning sight
        even after all these years
But that arc of brilliance in the sky
        now moves me to tears

Like you, it always dazzled me
        Nothing else could match it
And no matter how I played the game
        I never could quite catch it

Oh, I miss my garden of childhood
        where daydreams could come true
I still think about it often
        the rainbows, the daydreams, and you.

****

SPEED

What do you miss
as you rush through the day
in a frenzy to find what you need?

Would you recognize
the ultimate prize as you plow
through your life at top speed?

Did you ever regard the flowers
in your yard which were planted
in honor of you?

Did you hear your children sing
or see anything that they did
to receive praise from you?

Did you let love slip by because you
wanted a guy who would be
what you thought you required?

Now time has gone by and you
sit home and cry because you missed life
and now you're too tired.

****

HOME

I remember this place
from long ago;
I often laughed and played here
when flowers used to grow.

But where are all the roses
and the apple trees and vines?
Why are they replaced by stones
set in such perfect lines?

The flowers still are here, you say—
in bunches on each stone.
But no, they are not the same.
They don't grow on their own.

And there once stood a chicken coop,
a dark and dingy gray.
It held no chickens but the warmth
of children hard at play.

Now that's gone too and, in its place
a monument stands tall:
"To Mrs. B., symbol of love,
a mother to us all."

And I remember you—
you are the child of Mrs. B
Your eyes are warmth, your smile
is love, the way she used to be.

The other child, so secretly,
I loved him as did you.
What is this stone near Mrs. B's?
oh no—is he gone too?

I remember this place from long ago
as the only home I've known.
Away from here, I'm drifting—
angry, lonely, and alone.

Here was love and warmth and praise.
There was room here for me then.
Mrs. B, please take me home
Make room for me again.

✦✦✦✦✦✦✦

THAT'S LIFE

The grownups would gather
and talk a lot in muted whispers
behind cupped hands about
matters they wouldn't explain.
There was laughter, lots of sighs,
sometimes tears; and often
someone said, "That's life."

I wondered what that meant as
I waited for "life" to happen
and in the interim, I did as I was told.
I went to school, learned proper
spelling, mathematics, history
of the world, a little about a lot of things
but not much about life.

There were friends and parties;
I learned to dance, to kiss—
more fun than mathematics.
I also learned not everyone is kind,
and I learned to forgive,
though not always.

Later, when I went off to college,
some of my friends went off to war.
Not all came back, and I learned to cry—
grown-up tears, and I no longer
saw the world through a child's eyes.

I married and had children of my own.
I tried my best to answer their questions
but there were times I couldn't
especially about unfixable issues
and in those instances, all I
think of to say was, "That's life."

******

NOT LONG AGO

We had no cares not long ago
    no grief to understand
The world was ours not long ago
    We held our mother's hand

We watched in awe the grown-up world
    and wished it were our own
We anxiously awaited it
    good Lord, had we but known

We knew the first time that we loved
    true pleasure and great pain
and though 'twas merely love we loved
    the feelings were the same

For friends in need, we found a way
    to help when times were bad
but when we were in need of friends
    there were none to be had

We had no cares not long ago
    how brave we were, how bold
The world was ours not long ago
    when we had hands to hold

******

REMEMBERING THE DAISY DAYS

As children, my best friend and I climbed
a grassy hill that seemed to kiss the sky
It was dotted with flowers
We thought when we reached the top
the clouds would be just within our reach.

Along the way we passed some trees—giant
oaks and maples and a lone weeping willow.
And there were birds—bluebirds and robins
and we thought, "This is where they learn to sing"

Once at the top, we'd sit in the cool grass and pick
honeysuckle and drink nectar from the stems
We held buttercups to each other's chins
to see the bright yellow reflection on our faces

And then of course there were the wild daisies
which swayed in the grass and called for us
to pick one to determine whether the boys we liked
liked us back—he loves me, he loves me not.

Now all grown up I wander through a field
of flowers and stoop down to pick a daisy.
I gaze at this lovely, perfect flower, which seems
to stare right back at me with its big yellow eye.

Reminded as I am, of those carefree daisy days,
I look around, find myself alone, and begin
one by one to gently pull petals until
the last petal is gone: "He loves me not."

He loves me not? I glare in disbelief at that
unblinking yellow eye and with childlike
petulance, tearfully cry:
  "Is that your final answer?"
****

THE ROAD

I left behind the street of childhood
to navigate the highway of life,
exchanged dirt of backyard and joy
of sandbox for dust of the open road.

In a haze of youthful exuberance, I searched
for the adventure described in books.

I climbed mountains, crossed deserts,
sailed seas to cities and streets in lands
far and near; encountered life, both sweet
and simple, and also shockingly brutal
and barbaric and stood impotent,
in my naivete to do more than extend a hand.
Sometimes but only sometimes, that was enough.

I found joy and generosity in places
of dire need and deprivation,
sadness and selfishness in the midst
of opulence and plenty.

No longer do I walk carefree,
inhaling nature's bounty, but run, frantic,
in an endless quest for . . . HOME,
as I mourn the death of innocence
and damn the dawn of disillusion.

On this narrow track of time every now
becomes then in the blur of contemplation
of tomorrow. Yet, while each impediment
on this path may proclaim: this Road Leads
Nowhere, I find the fortune I believed this trip
would provide when I or anyone extends
a hand and sometimes that's enough.

****

ONE MAGIC NIGHT

In our last days of youthful innocence
while we protested a senseless war
in fear we would lose ourselves forever—
in those last days there were moments
of clarity and wonder which strayed
far beyond the bounds of imagination
to capture a memory so profound
that reality itself became suspect . . .
as on one magic night in the darkness
of the desert miles from the noise
and lights of the city when we gathered
among huge pillars of rock with nothing
but our guitars and our dreams.

We danced naked and free beneath the stars
with wanton abandon and in those seemingly
reckless moments as hands touched hands,
touched hearts touched heaven,
all that seemed lost was found.

Suddenly at the pinnacle of the tallest peak
there appeared a tiny brilliant point of light
and we watched in breathless wonder
as the silver blaze of the full moon
rose above us in silent splendor.

We held hands. We danced. We sang.
We played our music bathed unashamed
in celestial silver light as the magnificence
of those majestic moments imbued itself
forever into our memories.

My now heart relives with each rising
the gifts of that one magic night
and my dreams like the stars seem much closer
in the ethereal glow of moonlight.

******

HOLIDAY VISIT

In anticipation of your arrival
I bought new curtains for the guest room
cushy down comforters for the beds
Fresh flowers to match the curtains
were put on the dresser top

You—my most amazing creations
living breathing works of art
who took on lives of your own
just as intended, arrived like an
unexpected summer breeze
in the dead of winter
        and warmed me from the inside out

****

PANDEMIC ERA

PANDEMIC

The sur-reality of being the
only person walking the track
in the local park on a clear
sunny spring day makes me
wonder if this is how being
completely alone would feel.

I touch the mask covering my
nose and mouth, remind myself,
we're in the midst of a pandemic
and it's still early in the day; others
will be here soon, hopefully, masked,
and carefully keeping appropriate
distance from one another.

My attention is captured by the
long uncut grass and the profusion
of wildflowers, tiny buds of pink
and lavender mixed in the dense
patches of green clover and yellow
dandelions, all growing wild and free
happily rippling in the breeze.

Sadly, one day soon it will all be
manicured when life gets back
to normal and once again man
decides for Mother Nature what
belongs, what does not.

I pluck a dandelion, gone to seed,
make a wish that the pandemic
ends, everyone is safe, we can
all be together again, and if it's

not too much trouble, please
let Mother Nature have her way
now and again.

I lift my mask, blow the delicate fronds
and watch them disburse, to wherever
good wishes go to get granted.

****

WHERE IS THE COUNTRY I LOVE?

Where is the country I love?
In this place called home,
death hangs in the air
like storm clouds.
One never knows when its rage
will strike a random innocent
with a virus, a bullet,
a rogue officer of the law.

Where is the country I love?
Why are the upholders
of the laws which guarantee
freedom and equal justice
replaced by utter arrogance
and flagrant mendacity.

Had aliens been watching
our slow, steady destruction,
and ignorant disregard
for life of all kinds
and then sent a virus
so that the life we knew
ceased or slowed?

Had they then watched
a rebirth of the beauty
so long forgotten—of grasses
and wildflowers left alone
to choose their own place?
Had they heard birds return to trees
and fallen in love with their songs
and decided we didn't deserve any of it?

And then from somewhere
in a distant universe while
we sulked, sequestered in our homes
in fear of what we could not see
after we'd mistreated all we could see
they came, the invisible beings
and they took it, my country.

They stole my country and left
in its place this shameful replica
filled with ugliness and hate
to force us to see the mournful
truth of our actions.

Is it possible that happened?

Where is the country I love?

****

INAUGURATION EVE 2021

I don't give a damn about politics
But I know it's how some folks get their kicks
It isn't that I completely ignore it
though I admit I simply abhor it

I'm aware of who's who, who's good, who's not
who's altruistic, who would be a despot
This year, ignoring it all has been difficult
with Covid-19 and an anti-democracy cult

Which brings me to why I'm writing this rhyme
I fear there will be an attempt to begrime
a day which should be a great celebration
of a new President's inauguration

The obvious need for a strong military presence
diminishes hope for our country's coalescence
That even the honor of our troops is in question
jangles my nerves and creates indigestion

It is surely not simply waxing patriotic
to cheer the exit of what seems a psychotic
quest for money and power over all
by one with no concern for people at all

So, I watch the day unfold in the morning and think
It's cocktail time somewhere as I sip a stiff drink

******

WHAT ENEMY SHOULD WE FEAR

For a brief moment in time
the world was beautiful again
a clear bright cloudless
blanket of magnificent azure
shown above

Flowers grew wild and rampant
A profusion of rainbow colors
studded tall green lush grass
Trees reached out their limbs
and danced in the cleanest air
they'd breathed in decades.

They welcomed birds which
had long ago abandoned them
and now infused music in their
hearts: the sweet "tweet"
of sparrows, the "coo-coo" of doves,
and, even the raw "caw" of crows.

All of it was a joyful gift from
Mother Nature to the world.
Animals came out of hiding
and freely roamed city streets
without fear of being hunted.
Sea life returned to long-deserted
waters of rivers, streams, canals
and oceans, no longer polluted
by the fuel and detritus of man's
construction.

All of Mother Nature's children smiled.
A viral pandemic swept the globe.

Humans were in hiding, individually
sequestered in their self-made prisons
and huddled unhappily in virtual
fear-filled boats while the natural world
reclaimed its health and thrived.

It was as if the earth had been returned
to its most glorious before—
before technology, before trains,
before automobiles, before airplanes,
before ships, before man—
before, before, before.

And while this magic materialized,
in a little corner of the globe, the
ever-wise leaders of man saw fit
to spend their billions to send
exploratory vehicles to outer space,
to Mars, to discover whether life
had ever existed there in past
millennia—far more important
to them than to find and fund ways
to ensure that life continues to exist
here on earth.

Is not man the enemy of man?

******

ZOOM

How is it possible that I'm
doing too much when due
to this pandemic I really
can't do much of anything.

I don't go anywhere except
for an occasional walk or to buy food
But I have Zoom—the savior;
and now it's gotten out of hand.

That lifesaver has stolen my life,
I can't leave my computer.
I Zoom with friends and family,
take classes, and attend meetings.

I watch performances
of song, dance, opera, theater.
At times I even perform myself.
Zoom has taken over my life.

So, I don a mask, go for a walk,
bask in the warmth of the sun,
the breeze through my hair
try to inhale the fragrance of flowers.

I make my way to a nearly empty park,
sit in the grass, look at the clear sky
and think, *blue but empty, like pandemic life.*
The wind parts branches of a big tree.

Suddenly, like magic, on this clear day
in bright sunlight, sheer as tissue paper
a full moon winks at me in that blank sky.
I watch it; speak to it.

As I sit quietly, cross-legged in the grass.
a furry squirrel stops and stands by my foot;
the little guy contentedly munches a nut
relaxed as can be, its curious eyes watch me.

"Mr. Rocket J., Esquire, I presume," I say.
The critter tilts its head, stops munching,
stands taller as if to say "At your service Ma'am"

I smile; the two of us sit together in the world.

****

THERE IS NO SILENCE

Something disturbed the cocoon
of aloneness, I had begun to appreciate—
all the time with myself necessitated
by the Pandemic sweeping the globe.

There was a tapping sound coming
from the window in my office. Rain.
I caught sight of wet streets glistening
in the light from the few windows still
lit in the building across the street
at 2:00 a.m.

But it wasn't the rain that disturbed
me. That annoying sound I heard
had surreptitiously insinuated itself
into my awareness, an incessant
ghostly whoosh which I now realized
had been perpetually present for some
time, particularly in the quietude
of late night when shadows of sleep
beckon, a time when a very certain
truth had made itself known:

There is no silence in silence.

What I hear during that time is not
water running through pipes in walls
or a truck rolling past in the street
below. Neither is it wind howling
through trees or the simple settling
of walls all of which are easily unheard.

This is a more subtle ever-present
essence, not unlike one's own heartbeat
heard sometimes when all else is quiet
but usually sublimated by the more
familiar buzz of daily life.

It could simply be MY unique sound—
unlike any other person might hear
and it portends some special secret
for me which will one day reveal itself
like the clarity that sometimes comes
in the dark behind closed eyes.

Perhaps it's like the constant whir
of a machine audible only when
something is hopelessly broken
which in this particular circumstance
would render total silence an untimely end.

Alternatively, and most likely, I've spent
entirely too much time alone with me.

****

I DIDN'T THINK I MISSED THEM

I didn't think I missed them, my friends,
people in general, during pandemic seclusion.
They were often right in front of me
almost daily on my computer screen
They sang, waxed poetic, and shared stories.

I loved listening to those animated torsos.
The poets in their neat little squares
wrapped their words around me,
warmed me with beauty in the world
or chilled with its ugliness—easier
to hear when delivered poetically.

And the vivacious vocalists and musicians
who cleverly managed to synch voice
with live music from one square to another—
how they entertained and made me smile.
I never even considered whether or not they
were clothed below their chests.

New faces from distant places joined
these on-screen meetings and became
friends I would not otherwise have met
and for whom I am grateful, which proved
the pandemic had a positive purpose.

All were constant. I was fine.
I didn't miss them,

Then doors to the world swung open
and it was safe to venture out, mingle
with actual flesh and bone people,

at animated gatherings—for poetry,
for music concerts with singing and

live musicians playing glorious music;
dancing with friends I adored,
and sharing meals in restaurants,
sharing conversations—sharing
sharing, sharing.

I didn't think I missed them.

But suddenly I was a child in a store,
raiding the racks for candy, struggling
to decide which one to fondle first.
After two years of surviving on a diet
of nothing but visual vittles, I was hungry,
starving for something more—

TOUCH!!—hugs from old friends and new,
physically feeling the ecstatic energy
emanating from each person up close
or even from across the room, energy
of which I had never before been aware.
I didn't think I missed them but wow,

    I was so wrong.

******

FINALE

THANK YOU FOR THE STUFF

Did I ever say . . .

Thank you for all the stuff you gave
for which I was expected to be grateful
You know, the stuff for which you assumed
we shared a desire.

We didn't but thanks for the giving—
of your love and caring and your effort
to fit me in your world, convinced
I wanted to be there.

It helped me find my way.

And, thank you for the stuff wrapped so tight,
in so much miscellaneous madness and red tape,
it's taken years to open, each discarded layer
bringing me closer to the real treasure inside.

Or, if it was me—wrapped so tight,
thank you for your patience,
for all that wrapping inadvertently
taught me where I belong—and where I don't

And thank you for saying "I love you,"
three simple little words I thought were
frivolous as "hi" or "'bye" but now know
were sincere if only at the moment
spoken, a vital lesson because
love is a moment-to-moment event

and it is those moments that bring
the true meaning of life to life
and make it all worthwhile.

So, thank you family, thank you friends
thank you all—for the stuff.

****

ABOUT THE AUTHOR

"I don't usually like poetry, but I love yours" is the compliment Judy Barrat keeps closest to her heart and one she hears quite often.

Judy started writing poetry and short fiction as a young teenager, in an attempt to create pictures with words in the way her grandfather, a fine artist, did with a paintbrush. She wrote short rhymes about places that would remind her of what she saw or about the way something made her feel. Her later and current writing is similarly a result of her observations of the world, its content, and people, and her desire to take you with her to destinations real or imagined and introduce you to people she encounters along the way, with a modicum of humor and a softening of the "tough" stuff and turning it to a more positive view. This often results in expressing actual and/or exaggerated autobiographic snippets of life.

Though this is Judy's first book of poetry, many of the poems contained in this collection have been published in magazines, journals, and anthologies. She has previously published <u>The Oak Tree Diaries and Other Stories</u>, a collection of short stories.

In 2014, as a result of her attendance at an open mic (for vocalists), she began to combine her poetry and stories with live instrumental jazz and blues, which led to her presentation of five lavishly praised sold-out shows, at a supper club in West Hollywood, in which she performed her poetry and stories with musical accompaniment and sometimes a vocalist, all weaving their magic around her words. She enjoys performing her work and continues to do so at open mic venues both online, locally and nationally, and live around Los Angeles.

******

www.ingramcontent.com/pod-product-compliance
Lightning Source LLC
Chambersburg PA
CBHW041302120726

48005CB00014B/1828